The US Libertarian Movement

Other Books of Related Interest:

Opposing Viewpoints Series

American Values

Government Gridlock

Religious Liberty

The Republican Party

At Issue Series

Negative Campaigning

Poverty in America

Should the Federal Income Tax Be Eliminated?

Should the Rich Pay Higher Taxes?

The Wealth Divide

Current Controversies Series

Immigration

Politics and Religion

Social Security

The Tea Party Movement

Women in Politics

"Congress shall make no law . . . abridging the freedom of speech, or of the press."

First Amendment to the US Constitution

The basic foundation of our democracy is the First Amendment guarantee of freedom of expression. The Opposing Viewpoints series is dedicated to the concept of this basic freedom and the idea that it is more important to practice it than to enshrine it.

The US Libertarian Movement

Michael Ruth, Book Editor

GREENHAVEN PRESS
A part of Gale, Cengage Learning

Farmington Hills, Mich • San Francisco • New York • Waterville, Maine
Meriden, Conn • Mason, Ohio • Chicago

Judy Galens, *Manager, Frontlist Acquisitions*

For more information, contact:
Greenhaven Press
27500 Drake Rd.
Farmington Hills, MI 48331-3535
Or you can visit our Internet site at gale.cengage.com

Articles in Greenhaven Press anthologies are often edited for length to meet page requirements. In addition, original titles of these works are changed to clearly present the main thesis and to explicitly indicate the author's opinion. Every effort is made to ensure that Greenhaven Press accurately reflects the original intent of the authors. Every effort has been made to trace the owners of copyrighted material.

LIBRARY OF CONGRESS CATALOGING-IN-PUBLICATION DATA

Names: Ruth, Michael (Book editor)
Title: The US Libertarian Movement / Michael Ruth, book editor.
Description: Farmington Hills, MI : Greenhaven Press, 2015. | Series: Opposing viewpoints | Includes bibliographical references and index.
Identifiers: LCCN 2015026914 | ISBN 9780737775341 (hardback) | ISBN 9780737775358 (paperback)
Subjects: LCSH: Libertarianism--United States. | BISAC: JUVENILE NONFICTION / Social Science / Politics & Government.
Classification: LCC JC599.U5 U7 2015 | DDC 320.51/2--dc23
LC record available at http://lccn.loc.gov/2015026914

Printed in the United States of America
1 2 3 4 5 20 19 18 17 16

Contents

Chapter 4: How Do Libertarians View Other American Issues?

Why Consider Opposing Viewpoints?

> *"The only way in which a human being can make some approach to knowing the whole of a subject is by hearing what can be said about it by persons of every variety of opinion and studying all modes in which it can be looked at by every character of mind. No wise man ever acquired his wisdom in any mode but this."*
>
> *John Stuart Mill*

In our media-intensive culture it is not difficult to find differing opinions. Thousands of newspapers and magazines and dozens of radio and television talk shows resound with differing points of view. The difficulty lies in deciding which opinion to agree with and which "experts" seem the most credible. The more inundated we become with differing opinions and claims, the more essential it is to hone critical reading and thinking skills to evaluate these ideas. Opposing Viewpoints books address this problem directly by presenting stimulating debates that can be used to enhance and teach these skills. The varied opinions contained in each book examine many different aspects of a single issue. While examining these conveniently edited opposing views, readers can develop critical thinking skills such as the ability to compare and contrast authors' credibility, facts, argumentation styles, use of persuasive techniques, and other stylistic tools. In short, the Opposing Viewpoints Series is an ideal way to attain the higher-level thinking and reading skills so essential in a culture of diverse and contradictory opinions.

In addition to providing a tool for critical thinking, Opposing Viewpoints books challenge readers to question their own strongly held opinions and assumptions. Most people form their opinions on the basis of upbringing, peer pressure, and personal, cultural, or professional bias. By reading carefully balanced opposing views, readers must directly confront new ideas as well as the opinions of those with whom they disagree. This is not to argue simplistically that everyone who reads opposing views will—or should—change his or her opinion. Instead, the series enhances readers' understanding of their own views by encouraging confrontation with opposing ideas. Careful examination of others' views can lead to the readers' understanding of the logical inconsistencies in their own opinions, perspective on why they hold an opinion, and the consideration of the possibility that their opinion requires further evaluation.

Evaluating Other Opinions

To ensure that this type of examination occurs, Opposing Viewpoints books present all types of opinions. Prominent spokespeople on different sides of each issue as well as well-known professionals from many disciplines challenge the reader. An additional goal of the series is to provide a forum for other, less known, or even unpopular viewpoints. The opinion of an ordinary person who has had to make the decision to cut off life support from a terminally ill relative, for example, may be just as valuable and provide just as much insight as a medical ethicist's professional opinion. The editors have two additional purposes in including these less known views. One, the editors encourage readers to respect others' opinions—even when not enhanced by professional credibility. It is only by reading or listening to and objectively evaluating others' ideas that one can determine whether they are worthy of consideration. Two, the inclusion of such viewpoints encourages the important critical thinking skill of objectively evaluating an author's credentials and bias. This evaluation will illuminate an author's reasons for taking a particular stance on an issue and will aid in readers' evaluation of the author's ideas.

It is our hope that these books will give readers a deeper understanding of the issues debated and an appreciation of the complexity of even seemingly simple issues when good and honest people disagree. This awareness is particularly important in a democratic society such as ours in which people enter into public debate to determine the common good. Those with whom one disagrees should not be regarded as enemies but rather as people whose views deserve careful examination and may shed light on one's own.

Thomas Jefferson once said that "difference of opinion leads to inquiry, and inquiry to truth." Jefferson, a broadly educated man, argued that "if a nation expects to be ignorant and free . . . it expects what never was and never will be." As individuals and as a nation, it is imperative that we consider the opinions of others and examine them with skill and discernment. The Opposing Viewpoints series is intended to help readers achieve this goal.

David L. Bender and Bruno Leone,
Founders

Introduction

> *"Libertarians are America's largest third party and won 12.5 million votes nationwide in 2014. In New Jersey and many other states, Libertarians are the only party whose voter base is growing."*
>
> —*Patrick McKnight, "Letter: Get to Know the Libertarian Party," NJ.com, May 1, 2015*

The word *libertarian* holds two meanings in today's United States. The lowercased word refers to the political philosophy that espouses liberty as the prime goal of all governments. This ideology dates to the Taoist philosophers of ancient China but became more prominent during the seventeenth- and eighteenth-century Age of Enlightenment, when European thinkers such as John Locke began advocating for limiting the role of governments in their citizens' personal lives. This philosophy later left an especially meaningful impression on the Founding Fathers of the United States, who established the country in 1776 based on the libertarian principles of individual freedom and a small central government.

The capitalized word *Libertarian* refers to a member of the Libertarian Party, the third largest political party in the United States after the Republican Party and the Democratic Party. Despite this moniker, however, the Libertarian Party has remained mostly on the fringes of American politics since its founding in 1971, with Libertarian candidates for public office usually garnering only paltry numbers of votes when facing off against more well-known Republicans or Democrats. However, according to the Libertarian Party's late founder, David Nolan, this has been the party's plan all along: to nominate candidates who, it was assured, could never defeat their more mainstream opponents but who could still use their national fame to educate the American people in libertarian ideology.

Nolan's own education in political philosophy began at an early age. Born in 1943 in Washington, DC, Nolan began reading the novels of Robert A. Heinlein and Ayn Rand as a young man, becoming heavily influenced by their support of individualism, the philosophy that upholds the inherent value of each singular human being. Nolan later studied political science at the Massachusetts Institute of Technology, where he organized an activist group supporting Republican Barry Goldwater for president of the United States in the 1964 election. Following Goldwater's defeat by Democrat Lyndon Johnson, Nolan himself began taking a more active role in national politics, drafting a constitutional amendment intended to abolish the federal income tax and mailing libertarian bumper stickers to recipients around the country. Nolan was attempting to spread awareness of his growing political movement that called for a small central government that did not trample its citizens' individual freedoms.

By 1971, the anger of Nolan and his political companions over what they saw as the US government's increasing power at the expense of the people's liberty had reached a breaking point. On August 15, Nolan and his political partners became furious as they watched a televised announcement by President Richard Nixon during which Nixon declared that the United States was introducing to its economy a series of wage and price controls. This only fueled Nolan's existing rage over America's continued war in Vietnam, which he believed to be not only morally wrong but also illegal.

Finally, on December 11, 1971, Nolan and seven other libertarians convened in a friend's home in Colorado Springs and declared the formation of the Libertarian Party, which was to encourage conservative and liberal collaboration on capitalism, limited government, free economic markets, and unhindered civil liberties for all Americans. In the summer of 1972, the party held its first national convention in Denver, where it nominated philosopher John Hospers and television and radio host Theodora "Tonie" Nathan as the first Libertarian candidates for the respective offices of president and vice president of the United States. Their ticket ultimately received one electoral vote, and Nixon was reelected president. The singular Libertarian vote, however, marked the first time a woman, Nathan, had ever received an electoral vote in a US presidential election.

The Libertarian Party's poor performance in 1972 set a precedent for the organization, as most Libertarian candidates for president, even into the early twenty-first century, failed to secure much more than 1 percent of the popular vote in each election. Some ideological Libertarians, however, have received more mainstream attention by running for office as Republicans. Such was the case for former Texas congressman Ron Paul, whose 1988 run for president as a member of the Libertarian Party had garnered 0.47 percent of the vote. He ran again, as a Republican, in 2008 and 2012; in each instance, he accumulated a small but highly devoted support base and, by his association with other, more orthodox Republican candidates, received a great deal of national media coverage. Paul's libertarian stances still forced him to the margins of the Republican Party, however, and in each election, Paul received only a dismal amount of Republican delegate support. Similarly, in 2012, Libertarian presidential nominee Gary Johnson received 1 percent of the popular vote.

Other libertarian-leaning Republicans experienced better luck in 2010. That year, Rand Paul of Kentucky, son of Ron Paul, and Mike Lee of Utah were elected to the US Senate, while Justin Amash was elected to represent Michigan's third district in the House of Representatives. In each of their respective tenures, Paul, Lee, and Amash worked to advance the civil liberties that they believed the ever-expanding federal government had been robbing from the American people. Issues supported by some or all three of these politicians included relaxed federal marijuana laws, the allowance of free markets without government interference, and the demilitarization of America's police. In 2015 Rand Paul began receiving even more national attention when he announced his intention to seek the Republican nomination for president of the United States.

Opposing Viewpoints: The US Libertarian Movement examines the issues currently facing American libertarians. Multiple authors from competing political philosophies debate these issues in chapters titled "What Is Libertarianism's Place in Contemporary America?," "What Are the Economics of American Libertarians?," "What Is the Libertarian Stance on Social Issues?," and "How Do Libertarians View Other American Issues?"

What Is Libertarianism's Place in Contemporary America?

Chapter Preface

In the 2010s, US libertarianism, the political philosophy that supports a small national government and strong civil liberties for all individuals, has come to enjoy a place on the mainstream political stage through such nationally recognized federal legislators as retired Texas congressman Ron Paul; his son, Senator Rand Paul of Kentucky; and Congressman Justin Amash of Michigan. However, while these individuals and their ideas have received much of the American public's direct attention, another powerful libertarian force exists mostly outside the scope of the contemporary media fray, influencing the country's politics from the sidelines. This force is the Koch brothers, billionaires Charles and David, who for many years have advocated for and contributed hundreds of millions of dollars to libertarian-leaning Republican political efforts while mostly avoiding the news spotlight themselves.

Charles Koch, born in 1935, began earning his fortune in 1967, when he became chairman and chief executive officer of Rock Island Oil and Refining, the oil company founded by his father, Fred Koch. Charles renamed the enterprise Koch Industries in 1968 and subsequently began expanding into numerous other areas such as natural gas, fertilizers, plastics, and ranching. Charles's brother David, born in 1940, later became Koch Industries' executive vice president. In the twenty-first century, Koch Industries is one of the largest private corporations in the United States, boasting yearly revenues of $115 billion.

The American media, however, devotes substantially more attention to the Koch brothers' political activities than to their business. Both Charles and David have endeavored to promote a libertarian brand of Republicanism in the United States since their early years as the heads of Koch Industries. In 1977 Charles Koch cofounded the libertarian think tank the Cato

Institute in Washington, DC. This organization is dedicated to devising and advocating for public policies such as a limited central government, a free market economy unencumbered by government interference, guaranteed civil liberties for all Americans, and nonintervention in the affairs of other countries.

The brothers also contribute to a number of libertarian organizations and political advocacy groups such as the Reason Foundation, a libertarian research group that publishes conservative-minded opinions and articles through such outlets as *Reason* magazine and Reason.com; and the Institute for Humane Studies, a nonprofit organization that awards grants, scholarships, and prizes to entities that work to further the libertarian ideology in the United States.

Aside from simply contributing to these and other groups, David Koch himself ran for vice president of the United States, as the running mate of Ed Clark, in the 1980 election as a member of the Libertarian Party. The political positions Koch and Clark supported included the abolishment of Social Security, Medicare and Medicaid, public schools, a majority of American taxes, the Federal Bureau of Investigation, and the Central Intelligence Agency—all with the goal of removing the federal government from people's everyday lives. The Libertarian ticket eventually secured 1 percent of the popular vote in the election.

In the twenty-first century, though neither of the Koch brothers has again participated directly in politics themselves, their political activism and donations have only increased from years past. In the 2012 elections, the brothers and their organizations and political partners contributed a total of $400 million to efforts to elect Republican Mitt Romney as president and various other conservatives to the US Congress.

The Kochs' efforts ultimately failed, as Democratic incumbent Barack Obama was reelected in 2012, but their support of Romney still generated controversy among Democrats and other liberals, who accused the brothers of attempting to buy the election with their enormous fortune and political influence. These objectors also claimed that the Koch brothers were not even true libertarians, as they supported only those government policies that benefited themselves and other corporations like theirs. Real libertarians, critics claimed, would oppose corporatism in favor of equality for all, including the very poorest Americans. The Kochs' political activities made national attention again in 2015 when the brothers and their political partners set a donation budget of $889 million to elect a Republican in the 2016 presidential race.

The following chapter features a variety of authors examining the place of libertarianism in contemporary American politics and society. Subjects discussed in this chapter include the growth of libertarianism in America, whether the ideology improves or damages the country, the relationship of libertarianism to various other American political ideologies, and whether the libertarian form of populism benefits the American people.

Viewpoint 1

"From wanting to privatize health care, to doing away with federal agencies and eliminating minimum wage laws, libertarianism put the interests of billionaires and the wealthy elite first."

Libertarianism Is Bad for America

Daily Take Team

In the following viewpoint, the Daily Take Team argues that libertarianism is the wrong course for the United States. The political movement favors taking from the poor to give to the wealthy, the author writes, as billionaires wish to claim no responsibility for their own society. For this overarching reason, the author believes supporting libertarian candidates for office is a grave political mistake. The Daily Take Team is the writing staff of the Thom Hartmann progressive radio program.

As you read, consider the following questions:

1. What does the author's research claim would happen to insurance company stocks if Medicare were privatized?

Daily Take Team, "You Don't Know What 'Libertarian' Means," Truth-out.org, August 28, 2014.

2. What problem does the author have with the libertarian stance on American education?
3. What does the author claim will happen if libertarians eliminate the Food and Drug Administration?

If you want to know what libertarianism is all about, don't ask a libertarian, because most of them don't know.

A new poll from Pew Research [Center] found that only 11 percent of those surveyed who identified themselves as libertarian were correctly able to identify the very basic meaning of libertarianism as "someone whose political views emphasize individual freedom by limiting the role of government."

Even though that's often an oxymoron, that's what libertarians say, and their followers apparently don't know it.

Weirdly, that same poll found that 41 percent of libertarians believe that the government should regulate business, 46 percent of libertarians believe that corporations make too much profit, and 38 percent of libertarians believe that government aid to the poor is a good thing.

Similarly, of the so-called libertarians polled, 42 percent believe that police should be able to stop and search people who "look like criminals," and 26 percent think "homosexuality should be discouraged."

What happened to limited government and more individual freedoms?

Basically, people in America who call themselves libertarians have absolutely no idea what libertarianism is really about.

So, let's go over it for a second.

Pro-Billionaire

Back in 1980, David Koch, one half of the Kochtopus, ran as the Libertarian Party's vice-presidential candidate.

And the platform that he ran on back in 1980 provides a great summary of what libertarianism is really about.

First, libertarians want to "urge the repeal of federal campaign finance laws, and the immediate abolition of the despotic Federal Election Commission."

In other words, they want to make it as easy as possible for corporations and wealthy billionaires to flood our democracy with corruptive cash and buy even more politicians.

They want *Citizens United* [referring to the Supreme Court case of *Citizens United v. Federal Election Commission*, a decision that stated that corporations and other special interest groups have a constitutional right to spend as much as they want to elect a particular candidate] on steroids—and then some.

Next up, libertarians "favor the abolition of Medicare and Medicaid programs."

Instead, they want to privatize health care in America, so that their billionaire friends in the health care industry can get even richer, while working-class Americans are getting sicker and sicker.

In fact, a 2012 analysis by Citigroup found that insurance company stocks would skyrocket if Medicare alone were to be privatized.

And Big Pharma [pharmaceutical industry] would experience a revenue and profit boom, too.

Just look at America's experiences with Medicare Part D.

A report released by the House of Representatives back in July of 2008 found that, two years into the Medicare Part D experiment, American taxpayers were paying up to 30 percent more for prescriptions under the privatized part of the program.

And thanks to Medicare Part D, between 2006 and 2008 alone, drug manufacturers took in an additional $3.7 billion that they wouldn't have gotten through drug prices under the public Medicaid program.

Financial Concerns

Meanwhile, the 1980 libertarian platform also says that libertarians "favor the repeal" of an "increasingly oppressive" Social Security system.

They want to abolish Social Security, screw over working-class Americans, and take all the money that would go toward Social Security and invest it in Wall Street, so that their wallets can get even bigger.

There's over $2.5 trillion sitting in the Social Security Trust Fund right now.

Imagine how much money the libertarian banksters could make skimming even a fraction of a percent off the top of that every year.

Similarly, because libertarians want to hold on to their money and get even richer, they also "oppose all personal and corporate income taxation, including capital gains taxes."

They don't want to have any responsibility for society. Screw society!

Naturally, libertarians also think that "all criminal and civil sanctions against tax evasion should be terminated immediately."

According to Demos, in 2010, tax evasion cost the federal government $305 billion.

Imagine what America could have done with that $305 billion.

But, if you're rich, you shouldn't have to pay any taxes under libertarianism.

Next up, libertarians want to repeal laws that affect "the ability of any person to find employment, such as minimum wage laws."

In other words, "Screw the workers! We're the billionaires and we don't give a damn about workers!"

Education and Health

According to the 1980 platform, libertarians are also for the "complete separation of education and the state" and think that "government ownership, operation, regulation, and subsidy of schools and colleges should be ended."

Who cares about Thomas Jefferson and the University of Virginia, or Abraham Lincoln's land-grant colleges?

Screw public education! Poor people don't need to know how to read! Only rich people should be going to college, and billionaires can pay for their own kids' education!

And when they're done attacking public education in America, libertarians want to abolish the Environmental Protection Agency.

After all, pollution can be so profitable. And who cares if a few million people get asthma or die of cancer? They're not rich people! Screw them.

A 2010 study found that between 2005 and 2007, around 30,000 hospital trips and emergency room visits could have been avoided in California alone if federal clean-air standards had been met. Instead, those visits led to approximately $193 million worth of health care expenses for the American people.

Guess who benefited from that $193 million?

Transportation and Safety

Similarly, the 1980 platform makes it clear that libertarians also want to get rid of the Department of Energy, and close down any government agency that's involved in transportation.

No more standards for our roads, no more standards for our railways, no more standards for our airlines. Turn it all over to the billionaires. They can run it all and make a buck while they're at it!

And libertarians want to privatize our public highways and turn them all into toll roads too.

Wealthy Libertarians

The cult of the libertarian-minded ultra-wealthy would make an intriguing anthropological case study. But it would be a case study with a twist: Its research subjects increasingly control our economy, our politics, and even our personal lives. . . .

John Mackey, CEO [chief executive officer] of Whole Foods, is one of the nation's most visible "free-market libertarians." Mackey said this about government, and specifically about Obamacare [referring to the Patient Protection and Affordable Care Act], last year [2013] on NPR:

> "In fascism, the government doesn't own the means of production but they do control it and that's what's happening with the health care program with these reforms and so I'd say the system is becoming more fascist."

Presumably that means that the privatization of government services, an effort that includes every major defense contractor in this country, is a "fascist" scheme. We haven't heard Mackey make that argument, however.

The "fascist" government Mackey despises provides a number of services which have helped make him very wealthy. The USDA [US Department of Agriculture] certifies that the food sold in his stores is organic. Government built and maintains the roads and rails which bring Mackey's goods to each of his far-flung stores. Government regulators ensure that his stores' food is grown, prepared, packaged, and shipped in a manner that is safe and disease-free. Without government, John Mackey would still be running a little hippie store in Austin.

Richard Eskow, "5 Obnoxious Libertarian Oligarchs Who Earned Fortunes from the Government They'd Like to Destroy," AlterNet, Feb. 5, 2014.

So, if you want to drive to work you have to pay the Koch brothers!

Libertarians also want to do away with the Food and Drug Administration and the safety standards that agency imposes, so that Big Pharma and Big Ag [farming conglomerates] can make even more money, while you and I are forced to deal with the consequences.

Billionaires don't have to worry if their food is safe. They can own their own farmland, and hire their own cheap labor to work it!

Along those same lines, the 1980 platform says that libertarians want to get rid of the Consumer Product Safety Commission.

After all, if a kid is choking to death on some badly made cheapo toy, it's almost certain that it's a poor or working-class kid. One less moocher!

The 1980 libertarian platform also called for the repeal of the Occupational Safety and Health Act.

Right.

Workers don't need protections. Employers can just be trusted to keep their employees who are working for minimum wage safe.

The Poor and Minorities

Finally, libertarians "oppose all government welfare, relief projects, and 'aid to the poor' programs," claiming that these programs are, "privacy-invading, paternalistic, demeaning, and inefficient."

Or, in other words, turn poverty over to the rich people. After all, they've always done such a great job taking care of poor people. . . .

And, while it wasn't explicitly in the 1980 platform, who can forget that libertarians are also opposed to the Title II of the Civil Rights Act which, "prohibits discrimination because of race, color, religion, or national origin in certain places of public accommodation, such as hotels, restaurants, and places of entertainment."

To add insult to injury, they're also opposed to Title VII of the Civil Rights Act, which prohibits employers from discriminating based on race, color, religion, sex and nationality.

Who needs civil rights anyway?

Clearly, libertarianism is not what most Americans think it is.

From wanting to privatize health care, to doing away with federal agencies and eliminating minimum wage laws, libertarianism put the interests of billionaires and the wealthy elite first, and the interests of everyone else dead last. And I do mean dead.

Now, ask yourself, is that the America you want to live in?

I sure don't.

Viewpoint 2

> *"We, the members of the Libertarian Party, challenge the cult of the omnipotent state and defend the rights of the individual."*

Libertarianism Is Good for America

Libertarian Party

In the following viewpoint, the Libertarian Party contends that its various political policies will lead to increased personal freedoms and decreased power of the US federal government. These policies include the privatization of the health insurance market, the abolishment of the personal income tax, and the end of government involvement in all education. The Libertarian Party believes that societies that empower the individual over government are the best suited to succeed. The Libertarian Party of the United States was founded in the early 1970s.

As you read, consider the following questions:

1. What does the Libertarian Party say has been the problem with governments throughout history and all other American political parties?

Libertarian Party, "Libertarian Party Platform," lp.org, June 2014.

2. What is the Libertarian Party's position on private property?
3. What change does the Libertarian Party support making to the US Constitution as it relates to economics?

As Libertarians, we seek a world of liberty; a world in which all individuals are sovereign over their own lives and no one is forced to sacrifice his or her values for the benefit of others.

We believe that respect for individual rights is the essential precondition for a free and prosperous world, that force and fraud must be banished from human relationships, and that only through freedom can peace and prosperity be realized.

Consequently, we defend each person's right to engage in any activity that is peaceful and honest, and welcome the diversity that freedom brings. The world we seek to build is one where individuals are free to follow their own dreams in their own ways, without interference from government or any authoritarian power.

In the following pages we have set forth our basic principles and enumerated various policy stands derived from those principles.

These specific policies are not our goal, however. Our goal is nothing more nor less than a world set free in our lifetime, and it is to this end that we take these stands.

Statement of Principles

We, the members of the Libertarian Party, challenge the cult of the omnipotent state and defend the rights of the individual.

We hold that all individuals have the right to exercise sole dominion over their own lives, and have the right to live in whatever manner they choose, so long as they do not forcibly interfere with the equal right of others to live in whatever manner they choose.

Governments throughout history have regularly operated on the opposite principle, that the state has the right to dispose of the lives of individuals and the fruits of their labor. Even within the United States, all political parties other than our own grant to government the right to regulate the lives of individuals and seize the fruits of their labor without their consent.

We, on the contrary, deny the right of any government to do these things, and hold that where governments exist, they must not violate the rights of any individual: namely, (1) the right to life—accordingly we support the prohibition of the initiation of physical force against others; (2) the right to liberty of speech and action—accordingly we oppose all attempts by government to abridge the freedom of speech and press, as well as government censorship in any form; and (3) the right to property—accordingly we oppose all government interference with private property, such as confiscation, nationalization, and eminent domain, and support the prohibition of robbery, trespass, fraud, and misrepresentation.

Since governments, when instituted, must not violate individual rights, we oppose all interference by government in the areas of voluntary and contractual relations among individuals. People should not be forced to sacrifice their lives and property for the benefit of others. They should be left free by government to deal with one another as free traders; and the resultant economic system, the only one compatible with the protection of individual rights, is the free market. . . .

Economics and Resources

Libertarians want all members of society to have abundant opportunities to achieve economic success. A free and competitive market allocates resources in the most efficient manner. Each person has the right to offer goods and services to others on the free market. The only proper role of government in the economic realm is to protect property rights, adjudicate disputes, and provide a legal framework in which voluntary trade is protected. All efforts by government to redistribute wealth, or to control or manage trade, are improper in a free society.

We support a clean and healthy environment and sensible use of our natural resources. Private landowners and conservation groups have a vested interest in maintaining natural resources. Pollution and misuse of resources cause damage to our ecosystem. Governments, unlike private businesses, are unaccountable for such damage done to our environment and have a terrible track record when it comes to environmental protection. Protecting the environment requires a clear definition and enforcement of individual rights in resources like land, water, air, and wildlife. Free markets and property rights stimulate the technological innovations and behavioral changes required to protect our environment and ecosystems. We realize that our planet's climate is constantly changing, but environmental advocates and social pressure are the most effective means of changing public behavior.

While energy is needed to fuel a modern society, government should not be subsidizing any particular form of energy. We oppose all government control of energy pricing, allocation, and production.

All persons are entitled to keep the fruits of their labor. We call for the repeal of the income tax, the abolishment of the Internal Revenue Service and all federal programs and services not required under the U.S. Constitution. We oppose any legal requirements forcing employers to serve as tax collectors. Government should not incur debt, which burdens future generations without their consent. We support the passage of a "Balanced Budget Amendment" to the U.S. Constitution, provided that the budget is balanced exclusively by cutting expenditures, and not by raising taxes. . . .

Education and Services

Education is best provided by the free market, achieving greater quality, accountability and efficiency with more diversity of choice. Recognizing that the education of children is a parental responsibility, we would restore authority to parents to determine the education of their children, without interference from government. Parents should have control of and responsibility for all funds expended for their children's education.

We favor a free market health care system. We recognize the freedom of individuals to determine the level of health insurance they want (if any), the level of health care they want, the care providers they want, the medicines and treatments they will use and all other aspects of their medical care, including end-of-life decisions. People should be free to purchase health insurance across state lines.

Retirement planning is the responsibility of the individual, not the government. Libertarians would phase out the current government-sponsored Social Security system and transition to a private voluntary system. The proper and most effective source of help for the poor is the voluntary efforts of private groups and individuals. We believe members of society will become more charitable and civil society will be strengthened as government reduces its activity in this realm. . . .

Discrimination and Self-Discrimination

Libertarians embrace the concept that all people are born with certain inherent rights. We reject the idea that a natural right can ever impose an obligation upon others to fulfill that "right." We condemn bigotry as irrational and repugnant. Government should neither deny nor abridge any individual's human right based upon sex, wealth, ethnicity, creed, age, national origin, personal habits, political preference or sexual orientation. Members of private organizations retain their rights to set whatever standards of association they deem appropriate, and individuals are free to respond with ostracism, boycotts and other free market solutions. Parents, or other guardians, have the right to raise their children according to their own standards and beliefs. This statement shall not be construed to condone child abuse or neglect.

Whenever any form of government becomes destructive of individual liberty, it is the right of the people to alter or to abolish it, and to agree to such new governance as to them shall seem most likely to protect their liberty.

Our silence about any other particular government law, regulation, ordinance, directive, edict, control, regulatory agency, activity, or machination should not be construed to imply approval.

Viewpoint 3

> *"America clearly is becoming more libertarian—it's just that the transformation is happening in morality and culture."*

Yes, the Libertarian Moment Has Arrived

Damon Linker

In the following viewpoint, Damon Linker argues that the United States is currently undergoing a libertarian revolution, not in the political sense but through new morality and societal norms. Cultural stigmas on certain behaviors no longer hold any power, Linker writes, as individual Americans claim to be able to do anything they want with their own lives, without shame, as long as their actions do not negatively affect others. Damon Linker is senior correspondent for the Week *newsmagazine.*

As you read, consider the following questions:

1. What does Linker say are the attributes of the Democratic Party that attract younger voters?

Damon Linker, "Yes, the Libertarian Moment Has Arrived," *The Week*, August 13, 2014.

2. According to Linker, which US Supreme Court decision struck down the core of the federal ban on gay marriage?
3. What exception does Linker say Americans still make in regard to their refusal to submit to any higher authority?

Robert Draper posed an important question in last weekend's *New York Times Magazine* cover story: Has the "libertarian moment" finally arrived, with voters ready to support a presidential candidate (presumably Republican Rand Paul) who champions libertarian ideas? Those would include drastic cuts in taxes and spending, an end to the culture war and the war on drugs, and a foreign policy of much greater restraint than even Barack Obama has proposed and enacted.

A range of critics—from Jonathan Chait and Paul Krugman on the center-left, to David Frum on the center-right—have answered the question with a resounding "No!"

The evidence for their case, based mostly on surveys of public opinion, is strong. The American people on the whole support raising taxes on the wealthy. Young people are the most pro-government of any age cohort. Older Americans, by contrast, say they dislike government in the abstract, but even they favor the specific programs that benefit them directly. (Today those programs include Social Security and Medicare; someday soon Obamacare may join them.)

All of it adds up to an electorate in which older voters lean toward the Republican Party (anti-government rhetoric combined with social conservatism, tax cuts, and robust spending on the elderly) and younger voters favor the Democrats (social liberalism, tax hikes on the wealthy, and robust spending on everyone who asks for it).

Libertarianism, meanwhile, is nowhere to be found. Or rather, it remains what it always has been: a quirky, syncretic, marginal ideology with little mainstream political appeal.

There's just one problem: America clearly *is* becoming more libertarian—it's just that the transformation is happening in morality and culture, not in economic, tax, and regulatory policy.

The swift and broad-based triumph of the movement for gay marriage and the rapid rise in acceptance of marijuana legalization are the most obvious examples. But the source of these changes is deeper than the policies themselves—and may lead to other changes down the road.

The prophet of the moral and cultural libertarianism that is sweeping the nation may well be Supreme Court justice Anthony Kennedy, whose words upholding the right to abortion in *Planned Parenthood v. Casey* (1992) expressed an outlook that was just beginning to emerge 22 years ago, but which has since become common sense to many Americans: "At the heart of liberty is the right to define one's own concept of existence, of meaning, of the universe, of the mystery of human life."

Justice Antonin Scalia recognized immediately that such a libertarian principle created serious problems for morals legislation of any kind. In his *Casey* dissent, he pointed out that the principle would seem to make laws against bigamy unconstitutional.

Twelve years later, in *Lawrence v. Texas* (2004), Kennedy used similarly libertarian language to declare anti-sodomy laws unconstitutional—and Scalia was back to say that once all consenting adults, gay and straight, were free to do whatever they wished in the bedroom without any government interference, laws against same-sex marriage, adult incest, prostitution, masturbation, adultery, fornication, bestiality, and obscenity were bound to be thrown out as well.

The feud between Kennedy and Scalia has continued right down to *U.S. v. Windsor* (2013), which struck down the core of the federal ban on gay marriage, the Defense of Marriage Act. Kennedy once again based his majority opinion on (among other things) the liberty of homosexuals to make

Libertarianism Is Growing

Is the libertarian message winning? Coasting toward a major electoral victory next week, freedom-friendly Congressman Justin Amash certainly thinks so—even if Washington, D.C., isn't listening yet.

The libertarian Republican, who hails from a right-leaning district in western Michigan, is widely expected to win reelection on November 4. [Editor's note: Amash did indeed win reelection to a third term in 2014.] He already passed the real test: a significant primary challenge from a well-funded opponent backed by neoconservative and corporatist critics of Amash's views. . . .

"It felt great to get a big win," Amash told *Reason* in an interview. "The people of the district came out and said they like what I am offering, which is independent conservative representation, libertarian representation. . . . My challenger was offering run of the mill, establishment big government Republicanism. People are tired of that."

Amash is optimistic that what's true for his district is true for the country at large. A growing cross-partisan swath of the electorate is concerned about issues near and dear to the hearts of libertarians, including police brutality, spying, and drone warfare. . . .

First elected to Congress during the Tea Party wave of 2010, Amash says subsequent elections brought more representatives who are sympathetic to the views of an increasingly libertarian electorate into the fold.

"Our pro-liberty caucus is growing every year," he said.

Robby Soave, "Rep. Justin Amash Says Americans Are Becoming More Libertarian—And Congress Will Too," Reason.com, October 29, 2014.

"moral and sexual choices" without government interference—while Scalia angrily argued in his dissent that Kennedy's libertarian arguments implied that state-level bans on gay marriage were constitutionally unjustifiable. Since then, lower courts have eagerly (and repeatedly) vindicated Scalia's reasoning by citing his dissent to strike down such bans.

But the logic of Kennedy's libertarianism not only transformed constitutional law. It also anticipated the direction of public opinion and American popular culture in striking ways.

Americans now inhabit a world in which increasing numbers of individuals find it difficult, if not impossible, to imagine submitting to rule by any authority higher than themselves on moral and religious matters. Sure, people continue to accept that one will be judged harshly and punished for violating another individual's consent (the only libertarian moral consideration). But beyond that? Don't be ridiculous.

Who are you—who is anyone—to judge my behavior?

That's the rhetorical question we increasingly pose to ourselves, our family members, our neighbors, our church leaders, and our fellow citizens as a way to put a stop to any conversation that threatens to veer into moral evaluation and condemnation.

Consider the phenomenon of Miriam Weeks (Belle Knox), the Duke University undergrad who's become a breakout celebrity (and something of a libertarian folk hero) for proudly admitting that she works as a porn actress to pay for her education.

Pornography is obviously nothing new. But what *is* new—aside from its easy and costless availability online in effectively infinite quantities and varieties—is the claim that we shouldn't judge Weeks' decision to earn a living by having sex for money and in public, which is often the subtext behind discussion of her job choice. At least when the discussion isn't explicitly framed to make her look like a saint for "empowering women and sex workers."

In our libertarian paradise, moral judgments are perfectly acceptable, as long as they praise and never blame.

And just in case you're inclined to object on feminist grounds to singling out Weeks as an example of moral libertarianism, here's a recent column (with accompanying author photo) posted at *Time* in which a man named Jim Norton (who describes himself as a "consummate john") proudly declares, "I'm not ashamed to pay for sex—and other men shouldn't be either."

This doesn't mean that every man in America is ready to proclaim in a public forum that he regularly and shamelessly pays for sex. But it does mean that we now live in a culture in which an author (and a mainstream newsmagazine and website) can foresee no negative consequences of making such a proclamation.

Yes, the libertarian moment has arrived. Just not in the precise sense that Rand Paul and his ideological compatriots anticipated.

VIEWPOINT 4

> *"Libertarianism seems to be little more than a topic for esoteric dinner conversations."*

Libertarianism Is Not Growing in America

SR Larson

In the following viewpoint, SR Larson contends that although the United States' current economic and political statuses appear strong, they truly are not, for the libertarian movement has failed to enact any substantive changes in American society. According to Larson, this is because the overbearing American government has not provided ample opportunity for libertarianism to flourish as a mainstream political platform. Larson is an economist and libertarian who writes for The Liberty Bullhorn *blog.*

As you read, consider the following questions:

1. What two reasons does Larson provide explaining why the American economy is not growing at a higher rate?

SR Larson, "Has Libertarianism Failed?," Libertybullhorn.com, March 9, 2015.

2. What does Larson identify as three major problems with China's economy?

3. What two economists does Larson claim laid the intellectual groundwork for the American libertarian movement?

In a four-part series I presented the current state of the U.S. economy. Overall, things look relatively good here: Growth is moderately good, private consumption is moderately healthy, business investments are stabilizing at a good rate, and government consumption and investment spending are under control.

Generally, the private sector of the U.S. economy is in fairly good shape. So what is there to complain about?

The Illusion of Strength

First of all, the growth rates that I refer to as "moderately good" are at least a full percentage point below what we should have at this stage of a recovery, even from a deep recession. There are reasons why we are not at higher growth, one of them being the kind of government spending that does not show up in GDP [gross domestic product]: entitlements. Another reason is the [Barack] Obama administration's affinity for regulations. Without big entitlements and invasive regulations, we could easily be growing at 3.5–4 percent per year.

Secondly, the biggest strength of the U.S. economy is relative, not absolute. As I continuously report on this blog, Europe is in a perennial state of stagnation and industrial poverty. The Chinese economy is in what looks like a relatively serious recession; add to that a real estate bubble that they still don't know how to handle and the growing trend of job migration from China to lower-cost countries like Vietnam. Japan is fledgling but not much more than that.

And third—well, there is always Obamacare [referring to the Patient Protection and Affordable Care Act]. . . . Fortunately it looks like that reform, well-intended as it was, is being reshaped into something more palatable and manageable. It takes time, though, and while the president understandably holds on to his trademark legislative achievement he, too, must come to the conclusion that not all is good in America's most complicated piece of legislation ever. When that happens, another ball and chain around the ankle of the American economy will fall off and allow free market capitalism to grow even bigger.

Bottom line: The U.S. economy is not very impressive when compared to itself a couple of decades ago, but at least from an international perspective it is the best place to be for job seekers, families and businesses.

A Failed Movement?

The big question is why we can't do better. What is holding us back? As a libertarian, my conclusion is "big government." As an economist, my conclusion is "it depends, but big government is a strong candidate." But that only begs another question: How is it that the United States, a constitutional republic born from the yearnings of freedom, has fallen for the temptation of the big welfare state?

This is a big question to answer. A good way to start is to ask what has happened to the most freedom-loving movement in recent American history—the libertarian movement—and why it has failed to turn the tide on big government. After all, modern libertarianism is now almost half-a-century old. The intellectual groundwork was laid in part by economists like Milton Friedman and Friedrich von Hayek (who, by the way, allegedly did not get along with one another) and partly by the great moral philosopher Robert Nozick. In his *Anarchy, State, and Utopia*, originally published in 1974, Nozick challenged the prevailing wisdom of redistributive justice and—by implication—the theoretical foundations of the welfare state. His vision of the minimal state was close in theory to the

Libertarianism Is a Flawed Ideology

When success itself is admired, regardless of how it is won, then the result becomes what the philosopher Thomas Hobbes called "the state of nature," in which there is "continual fear, and danger of violent death; and the life of man, solitary, poor, nasty, brutish, and short."

This is what results when everyone places success above fairness or any other ethical objective. Some people call this "state of nature" "libertarianism," or "anarchy," and they think that this might-makes-right society is the ideal form of "government" (no government at all), toward which the world should strive. . . .

This is the problem that libertarian believers must wrestle with, if they are at all serious, instead of just ideological kooks.

So, rejecting government solves nothing. It's like rejecting food: The real issue isn't to reject food, it's to eat healthful food, and to avoid poisonous food. Similarly, the real issue isn't to reject government, it's to support good government, and to oppose bad government.

And so, too, the issue isn't whether government should be "small," or "big," but rather that it should be the best size to serve the public, who must bear its costs.

In other words: Libertarianism entirely avoids the real question, which is: What type of government is good? As an "ideology," libertarianism doesn't even make it to first base: it's fake, from the get-go. That's why libertarianism fails.

Eric Zuesse,
"Libertarianism Is a Fundamentally Flawed Ideology,"
Business Insider, December 18, 2012.

small government that would be necessary for Hayek's and Friedman's free market capitalism to work.

The [Ronald] Reagan presidency marked a surge for libertarianism in America. Similarly, the [prime minister Margaret] Thatcher era unleashed libertarian thinking and activism in Britain. While its success on continental Europe was more limited, the libertarian movement made its footprints, especially in Scandinavia and Eastern Europe, where it helped inspire the liberation from the Soviet empire.

But what looked like a success story back then never translated into policy success. Why?

The question is highly relevant. In a world where government consumes 40 percent or more of GDP; when taxes can take away more than half of a man's earnings; when government controls or wants to control the education of all children and the health care of all citizens; in that world, libertarianism seems to be little more than a topic for esoteric dinner conversations.

Where are the libertarian victories? Can libertarianism even be saved?

Yes, it can. But only under some very important conditions. For more on this, check in tomorrow [at *The Liberty Bullhorn* blog].

VIEWPOINT 5

> *"Some liberals, fed up with Democratic waffling on issues like military intervention and corporate welfare, are finding something attractive in Republican Sen. Rand Paul's brand of libertarianism."*

Liberals Can Support Libertarians

Onan Coca

In the following viewpoint, Onan Coca argues that liberals should find some common political ground with the libertarian Republican senator Rand Paul. This is because Paul has taken numerous stances against problems he sees in his own Republican Party. According to Coca, these are issues that Democrats could naturally support as well. Coca is a news editor for Eagle Rising.com.

As you read, consider the following questions:

1. Of which decision of President Barack Obama's does Coca say Rand Paul questioned the legality?

Onan Coca, "Why Do Liberals Love Rand Paul?," EagleRising.com, November 18, 2014.

2. Which issue does Coca say Paul has also attacked in the Republican Party?
3. According to the viewpoint, how has the Democratic Party been losing votes to libertarians such as Paul?

Senator Rand Paul (R-KY) has long been under assault from the GOP [Grand Old Party, referring to the Republican Party] establishment who see the Kentuckian as too ideologically rigid.

Senator Paul teams well with Senators Ted Cruz and Mike Lee as well as having a close ally in Senate Majority Leader Mitch McConnell (R-KY). He has been attacked by squishy moderates like Rep. Peter King (R-NY) and liberal darlings like Senator John McCain (R-AZ).

So how is it that Senator Paul has become a fan favorite of many a disenchanted liberal? It has to be conviction.

Senator Paul speaks out against corporate welfare—but unlike many Democrats who do the same . . . Senator Paul means it. He speaks out against military intervention, for judicial reform and for social liberty but again, unlike Democrats, he means it.

Unifying Policies

Some liberals, fed up with Democratic waffling on issues like military intervention and corporate welfare, are finding something attractive in Republican Sen. Rand Paul's brand of libertarianism.

In an op-ed for *Huffington Post* on Monday [November 16, 2014], H.A. Goodman explained why, even though he identifies as "a liberal Democrat" and has "never voted for a Republican," he plans to vote for Sen. Paul in the 2016 presidential election.

"On issues that affect the long-term survival of this country," Goodman says, "Rand Paul has shown that he bucks both the Republican and Democratic penchant for succumbing to public opinion, an overreaction to the terror threat, and a gross indifference to an egregious assault on our rights as citizens."

Goodman applauds Paul, for instance, for questioning the legality of President [Barack] Obama's decision to quietly increase troop deployments in Iraq amidst an ongoing bombing campaign against ISIS [an extremist militant group in the Middle East]. The deployment came "without a peep from the anti-war left," but as Goodman points out, "the reaction would have been entirely different from liberals throughout the country" if it had been made by a Republican president.

Moreover, "Paul is one of the few Republicans who's addressed the GOP's love affair with corporations," Goodman says, citing the senator's statement that, "corporate welfare should once and for all be ended."

And while he acknowledges the risk that Paul might flip-flop on some of those issues, Goodman notes that "Hillary Clinton and President Obama have changed their views on everything from gay marriage to marijuana legalization and Iraq."

Goodman even expresses skepticism that Clinton is "any more liberal than Paul on Wall Street or banking, although perhaps she'd be more willing to save failed corporations than the Kentucky senator."

Breaking from the Mold

Tim Donovan, a self-described "liberal hipster," echoed Goodman's sentiments in an op-ed for *Salon* on Monday, saying, "I'd vote for Rand Paul for president faster than you can say 'libertarian wacko' if I thought he would actually end the drug war, slash corporate welfare, and plow the savings into student loan debt relief or a robust infrastructure bill."

If even a committed partisan such as himself can consider ignoring party affiliation, Donovan says he "can only assume

Why Democrats and Libertarians Differ

The ancient debate of liberty vs. equality motivated the founders to undertake the endeavor of establishing the United States of America. In contemporary politics, this debate is often lost in the partisan bickering that is, quite frequently, the same point rephrased and repeated back. However, the growing Libertarian Party is the party of liberty and should they or their ideas rise to power, the Democratic Party would be free to once again infuriate Libertarians by setting themselves in opposition: standing for equality.

You see, the Libertarian Party and the Democratic Party already agree on a number of issues (regardless of the methods to achieve them). For instance, Democrats and Libertarians can agree that the war on drugs is a failure and has succeeded only in padding the pockets of participants in the "Prison-industrial-complex," or that peace is better than endless war. Obviously, this is not an exhaustive list, and there are many things that Libertarians and Democrats disagree about (social programs, size of government, etc.). . . .

By no means do I believe that Libertarians and Democrats of the future will be any less supportive of their respective views when they disagree. However, I do strongly believe that both parties would benefit from the growth of the Libertarian Party—and thus the return of its ideals to the American conscious.

Emory Babb,
"Frenemies: Why Democrats and Libertarians Are Like Oil and Vinegar," Mic, December 18, 2012.

that less ideologically committed millennials are even more willing to vote Republican for the right candidate or platform."

The main reason Donovan gives for considering such apostasy is that "Democrats are far too committed to being a centrist, business-friendly party," unwilling "to shed the yolk of Clinton-era conformity and compromise."

Donovan argues that, "Democrats have failed to embrace the policies their voters clearly desire," allowing Republicans like Sen. Paul to steal a march on them with regard to themes like economic populism.

Russell Brand, the far-left British comedian, suggested in an interview with Democracy Now that the allure of candidates like Sen. Paul stems from the fact that they break from the traditional mold of politicians who are "only interested in servicing the needs of corporations."

Brand claimed that, "we live in a system where tax breaks and tax avoidance are easy if you understand the law," but because we also have "a media that's dominated by corporate interests . . . we can't just say aloud that we live under a feudal system, we live under an oligarchy."

VIEWPOINT

> *"Grassroots libertarians appear to place a far higher priority on the economic issues that bind them to the GOP than the social values they share with progressives."*

Progressives and Libertarians Should Ally but Never Will

Zack Beauchamp

In the following viewpoint, Zack Beauchamp contends that libertarians and progressives will never ally politically, even though they share many of the same views. Beauchamp claims that this is due to libertarians' refusal to engage with progressives about the social values on which both groups agree. Instead, Beauchamp writes, libertarians focus only on the economic issues that distance them from progressives. Beauchamp is a reporter for ThinkProgress *news blog.*

As you read, consider the following questions:

1. What does Beauchamp say is the one issue that has united libertarians more than any other?

Zack Beauchamp, "Why Libertarians and Progressives Will Never Get Along," Think Progress.org, October 30,2013.

2. What does Beauchamp say is unexpected about libertarians' positions on social issues in relation to Democrats?

3. On which two libertarian issues does Beauchamp say neither the libertarians nor progressives have taken the lead?

Unlike some progressives, I'm deeply sympathetic to the idea of a left-libertarian alliance. I like the libertarians' line on the drug war, mass incarceration, civil liberties, corporate welfare, immigration, and restrictions on Internet pornography and other infringements [of] free speech. Libertarians are a net-positive influence on Republican foreign policy and some of their arguments for economic freedom contain important insights about oppression and domination. There's a lot to recommend about "liberaltarianism," [liberal-libertarian combination] in short.

And yet it never seems to amount to anything in real terms. At the recent anti-snooping "Stop Watching Us" rally, a rare concrete instance of libertarian connection, former New Mexico governor Gary Johnson told BuzzFeed that libertarians were more naturally allied with progressives than mainline Republicans. So why did Johnson run for governor (and president, before he defected to the Libertarian Party) as a Republican?

A new poll released on Tuesday [in October 2013] squares the purported circle. Grassroots libertarians appear to place a far higher priority on the economic issues that bind them to the GOP [Grand Old Party, referring to the Republican Party] than the social values they share with progressives. As a consequence, they hate Democrats and on-balance like the GOP. It doesn't seem, in short, that American libertarians have much interest in building anything resembling a durable alliance with progressives.

Signs of the Gap

Public Religion Research Institute's [PRRI's] poll found that seven percent of the total American population were libertarians, as identified by their answers to a slate of nine broadly worded questions on foreign, economic, and social policy. Another 15 percent lean libertarian, so libertarian-ish Americans aren't a meaninglessly small slice of the electorate.

But they are a highly conservative, Republican one. 57 percent of libertarians identify as conservatives in the PRRI poll, while a scant three percent identified as liberals. 45 percent of libertarians identify as Republicans and 39 percent "identify with the Tea Party movement." 57 percent of libertarians have favorable views of the Republican Party, while a whopping 89 percent have unfavorable views of the Democratic Party.

Though people often assume libertarians vote third party or not at all, that doesn't appear to be true. Libertarians reported voting in primary elections at significantly higher levels than the general population, and a higher percentage of libertarians (80 percent) than white evangelicals (79 percent) supported Mitt Romney in the general election [of 2012]. Given that [Barack] Obama was no worse, and in all likelihood better, on social issues and foreign policy from a libertarian perspective, that's implicit evidence that libertarians tend to prioritize economic issues in their actual political [decisions].

As it happens, PRRI's poll also provides direct evidence. The one thing that united libertarians, more than anything else? Opposition to Obamacare [referring to the Patient Protection and Affordable Care Act]. An extraordinary 96 percent of libertarians had an unfavorable view of the law—eight points higher than the equivalent figure among self-identified Tea Partiers! Similarly, libertarians are more opposed to a minimum wage hike than Tea Partiers, while the two are equally inclined to oppose environmental regulations.

You might think libertarians would be similarly to the left of the Democratic Party on social issues, but that's not quite so. On the banner issues, marriage equality and abortion, libertarians are to the right of Democrats. A majority outright *opposes* same-sex marriage, while libertarians are 14 points less likely to oppose making access to abortion more difficult than Democrats.

Moreover, on the social issues where libertarians really are more permissive than Democrats, they're not as united as they are on opposition to Obamacare or distaste for the Democratic Party. For example, significantly more libertarians supported Mitt Romney for president than supported legalizing marijuana (80 percent to 71 percent, respectively).

Fundamental Differences

What to make of these numbers? First, grassroots libertarians just don't seem to share the priorities of libertarian intellectuals. While prominent libertarians often take a "pox on both their houses" approach to party politics, the libertarian movement's base appears to vote like partisan Republicans.

Given what we know about American political behavior, this isn't surprising. Americans basically don't vote on foreign policy absent a massive ongoing ground war, which means one potential point of libertarian comity won't end up mattering at the ballot box. Moreover, though many libertarians are registered independents, those folks basically all vote like partisans. Those well-established lines of research lend credence to the survey's baseline finding that there simply aren't many libertarians who flip back and forth between the parties.

Arguably, these libertarians are just being rational. Both parties are significantly more supportive [of] aggressive counterterrorism policy and civil liberties restrictions than libertarians would like, and neither party has taken the lead on libertarian issues like drug law reform or cutting corporate welfare out of the tax code. Even though Republicans are bad on a lot of economic issues, the line goes, they're still less statist than the Democrats.

On the other hand, you could just as easily imagine a different brand of libertarian making the reverse argument. A Republican Party dominated by neoconservatives can't be trusted not to start more disastrous wars, while Obama kept us out of Syria. The Republicans also want to use the power of the state to take away the rights of women and gays, our hypothetical liberaltarian would tell her right-libertarian friends, while Republicans have a proven track record of hollow promises on the deficit and entitlement reform. Some prominent libertarians, in fact, made similar arguments in 2008.

And yet, these libertarians just don't seem to exist in the wild. Rank-and-file libertarians, it seems, are virtually all right-libertarians, concerned with shrinking the state's economic footprint to the exclusion of other libertarian priorities.

A Premium on Economics

It's easy to see how this makes a libertarian-progressive alliance a pipe dream. Since libertarians don't have the numbers to out and out displace conservatives as the dominant right-leaning ideology in the United States, they'll have to operate inside the GOP coalition if they want to be involved in electoral politics.

But if libertarian voters place a premium on economics, they'll be willing to support Republican candidates who veer hard right on role-of-government questions despite their foreign belligerency and social authoritarianism, Romney being the case in point. That means you'll end up with comparatively few true libertarians like Rand Paul or Justin Amash, the kind of legislators who make temporary liberaltarian alliances possible on security and civil liberty issues, in office. You'll more likely see libertarians for Ted Cruz.

One final thing: The PRRI poll is just more evidence that, as much as people talk about the United States as being divided by social and foreign policy, it's the role of the state in the economy that really divides us. That's the fundamental fault line in American politics, and it explains why, as much as an alliance might make sense on some issues, progressives and libertarians will always end up on opposite sides of the political barricades.

VIEWPOINT 7

> *"Republicans can push a populist agenda that would slowly roll back the size and scope of the federal government, thus giving all Americans more freedom to prosper."*

Libertarian Populism Is Good for American Politics

Conn Carroll

In the following viewpoint, Conn Carroll contends that libertarian populism shows promise for American politics, as it responds to the American people's calls for economic equality for all. According to Carroll, this style of conservative populism vows to reform American taxes so the financial burden is lifted off the poor and placed on the wealthy, a change that would benefit the country as a whole. Carroll is White House correspondent for Townhall.com.

As you read, consider the following questions:

1. According to Carroll, what are the apparent benefits of American corporatism?

Conn Carroll, "The Case for Libertarian Populism," Townhall.com, July 1, 2014.

2. What tax does Carroll say is making working Americans poorer?
3. According to Carroll, what Republican reputation keeps millions of Americans from voting for the party?

Something is rotten in the United States of America.

Except for a brief surge of pride after the United States swore in its first black president in 2009, Americans have consistently told pollsters for more than a decade that they believe our country is heading in the wrong direction.

Neither party is offering an agenda that speaks to America's concerns.

Democrats only want to grow the size and scope of the federal government at a time when America's trust in its federal government has never been lower. Republicans want to cut taxes for the wealthy and help big corporations at a time when Americans believe federal government policies already favor the wealthy.

Americans want an alternative. An alternative that dismantles the power and wealth of special interests on the left and the right. An alternative that recognizes we can shrink the size and scope of the federal government in ways that benefit all Americans.

Some Republicans have recognized this need and are already advancing policies that move the party in this direction. But a wider agenda that adheres to these principles is possible. Let's begin by examining where the two major parties have gone wrong.

The Corporatist Democratic Party

For liberals, the source of Americans' unease is easily identifiable: income inequality.

It's what brought the Occupy movement [a group that protests against social and economic inequality] out into the streets. It's the subject of a wildly popular new book by French socialist Thomas Piketty. And President [Barack] Obama recently called it, "The defining issue of our time."

How do liberals plan to fight income inequality? Through higher taxes on the wealthy and a slew of new government programs to redistribute the money, of course.

But progressives realized long ago that they needed deep-pocket partners to help run and popularize their treasured government programs. As Bill Scher of the liberal Campaign for America's Future recently admitted in the *New York Times*, "The necessity of corporate support for, or at least acquiescence to, liberal policies is not a new development in the history of American liberalism. Indeed, it has been one of its hallmarks." . . .

The Failing Corporatist Model

For decades now, corporatism has been a big winner for both the Democratic and Republican Parties. In his recent book *Mass Flourishing*, 2006 Nobel Memorial Prize in Economic Sciences winner Edmund Phelps explains why:

> Corporatism satisfies a desire for security. People want security of consumption, security of jobs, and security of their economic status. Corporatism replaces the decentralized competition of the market with political control over the economy.

Corporatism allows CEOs [chief executive officers] to deliver near guaranteed steady profits while receiving fat salaries in return. It allows union leaders to promise lifetime jobs and generous benefits. And it allows politicians to take credit for every job, created or saved, by every company that takes a single dime from the government.

But corporatism no longer seems to be providing the peace of mind that it once did. According to a recent Pew [Research

Center] poll, the percentage of Americans who describe themselves as middle class has fallen from 53 percent in 2008, to 44 percent today.

Meanwhile, the percentage of Americans who describe themselves as "upper class" has also shrunk from 21 percent to 15 percent over that same time. Only the ranks of the self-described "lower class" are growing. Their numbers have almost doubled from 25 percent in 2008 to 40 percent today. . . .

Why Corporatism Fails

Corporatism can, and often does, thrive. But only for a limited time. Eventually the tools Big Business and Big Government use to maintain their monopoly on power, undermine economic growth. . . .

And the American people know the partnership between Big Government and Big Business is making their lives worse.

An October 2013 CNN poll found that while 60 percent of Americans agree with the statement that "the government is trying to do too many things that should be left to individuals and businesses," just 35 percent said "that government should do more to solve our country's problems."

A September 2013 Gallup poll found that 60 percent of Americans agree with the statement that the federal government has "too much power" while just 32 percent said it has "the right amount." . . .

The Libertarian Populist Alternative

At the same time that American distrust in the federal government is at record highs, there is also a strong populist streak running through the American people.

Sixty-four percent of Americans recently told ABC News that federal government policies currently favor the wealthy, while 57 percent said they'd support policies to try to reduce the wealth gap in this country.

And according to Bloomberg, 64 percent of Americans believe the country no longer offers everyone an equal chance to get ahead, while an even larger 68 percent believe the income gap between rich and poor is growing. Additionally, 52 percent of Americans think the government should redistribute wealth "by heavy taxes on the rich," while just 45 percent say it should not.

Republicans should not ignore these populist impulses. Rather, they should embrace them because the public is largely right. The current corporatist policies coming from Washington do favor the wealthy.

It is harder to get ahead in this country when entire sectors of the economy are controlled by a few highly regulated, government-favored firms. The tax code does contain far too many loopholes for the rich and powerful that subsequently drive up tax burdens on the rest of America.

By trying to do too much, and often advantaging the wealthy and politically connected in the process, the federal government has become a force for growing inequality and economic immobility.

Republicans need to find ways they can help the everyday lives of average Americans by cutting the size and scope of the federal government.

A Libertarian Populist Agenda

The federal government will spend $3.5 trillion in 2014 administering an unknown number of government programs through more than 500 government agencies using almost 2.8 million employees.

Not every wasteful program or agency can be identified in this short space, and it would be next to impossible to eliminate them all at once. But Republicans can push a populist agenda that would slowly roll back the size and scope of the federal government thus giving all Americans more freedom to prosper. Here are just some areas where they could start.

Give Every Working American a Raise

If you wanted to design a tax that both made working Americans poorer and killed jobs in the process, the 12.4 percent Social Security payroll tax is exactly what it would look like.

Almost one-quarter of all federal government revenue ($673 billion) was raised by the Social Security payroll tax in 2013, and it is one of the most regressive tax policies the federal government administers. . . .

If Republicans proposed limiting the mortgage interest deduction to just households with incomes below $200,000, and they eliminated the mortgage deduction for second homes, as well as the state and local tax deduction, the real property tax deduction, the state and local bond interest exclusion, and the investment income on life insurance exclusion, all of which predominately benefit wealthy households, they then could also cut the employee side of the payroll tax in half without adding a dime to the deficit.

Not only would that mean a smaller tax code and a less intrusive federal government, but it would also mean an extra $1,500 a year in take-home pay for the average American household. . . .

A New Republican Party

In 1976, President [Gerald] Ford narrowly lost the White House to former Gov. Jimmy Carter, 48 percent to 50 percent. Carter's narrow margin was secured by lower-income Americans who gave Carter an overwhelming 62 percent to 38 percent margin (two points worse than [Mitt] Romney's 2012 showing).

Just two months later, on February 6, 1977, a former governor of California told a packed hotel ballroom in Washington, D.C., that the Republican Party would have to reinvent itself if it was going to survive.

"The New Republican Party I envision will not be, and cannot be, one limited to the country club–Big Business image that, for reasons both fair and unfair, it is burdened with today," this former governor said.

"The New Republican Party I am speaking about is going to have room for the man and the woman in the factories, for the farmer, for the cop on the beat, and the millions of Americans who may never have thought of joining our party before, but whose interests coincide with those represented by principled Republicanism."

That former governor was, of course, President [Ronald] Reagan. And in the 1980 election, not only did Reagan beat Carter 51 percent to 41 percent, but he cut Ford's 24 point loss among the lowest-income Americans to just 10 points.

Republicans can win significant votes from every demographic. There are millions of Americans who share the Republican Party's limited government vision but just don't vote for them because Republicans have a reputation for supporting the rich and not caring about the poor.

By pursuing an agenda and crafting a message that demonstrates how a smaller government can help the everyday lives of average Americans, especially those with lower incomes who suffer from regressive payroll taxes and government subsidized debt, Republicans can win elections in presidential years again.

Periodical and Internet Sources Bibliography

The following articles have been selected to supplement the diverse views presented in this chapter.

Robert Draper	"Has the 'Libertarian Moment' Finally Arrived?," *New York Times*, August 7, 2014.
Micah J. Fleck	"7 Examples of How Liberals Misrepresent Libertarianism," *Libertarian Republic*, May 27, 2015.
Conor Friedersdorf	"Libertarians Can Be a Significant Force for Good in U.S. Politics," *Atlantic*, August 14, 2014.
David Frum	"Why the 'Libertarian Moment' Isn't Really Happening," *Atlantic*, August 11, 2014.
David Harsanyi	"Do Libertarians Have a Political Future? A Conversation with David Boaz," *Federalist*, May 8, 2015.
Edwin Lyngar	"My Personal Libertarian Hell: How I Enraged the Movement—and Paid the Price," *Salon*, March 30, 2015.
Neil Ross	"'People Can't Lead Full Lives If They're Dependent on the State,'" *Spiked*, May 29, 2015.
Jennifer Rubin	"Why Conservatives and Libertarians Are at Odds,'" *Washington Post*, September 11, 2014.
Jeffrey A. Tucker	"What a Principled Social Movement Looks Like," Foundation for Economic Education, February 24, 2015.
Anthony Zurcher	"Is Ferguson the Start of a 'Libertarian Moment,'" BBC News, August 14, 2014.

Chapter 2

What Are the Economics of American Libertarians?

Chapter Preface

A substantial portion of American libertarian thought relates to money and the economy. Libertarians staunchly oppose any powerful central government that becomes involved in the private financial sector of a country; to them, not only does this constitute a gross misuse of government authority, but it also results in nearly irreparable financial damage to millions of citizens when the government's economic tactics fail. Therefore, advocating for a free market economy, in which producers and consumers agree on the prices of goods and services without government oversight of any kind, has become one of the main talking points of American libertarians running for public office in the twenty-first century.

This issue became especially prominent in the 2010s, in the immediate aftermath of the recession. This was the period from 2007 to 2009 in which economic markets around the world suddenly and severely declined, leading in many cases to the financial ruin of numerous large corporations. In the United States, the financial and automotive sectors of the economy were especially hard-hit by the recession, requiring government bailouts in 2008, under President George W. Bush, and 2009, under President Barack Obama.

These bailouts became prime political fodder for libertarian-minded Republicans such as US congressman Ron Paul of Texas, who, in accordance with the traditional libertarian position, proclaimed that the federal government possessed no right to use American taxpayers' money to save corporations that only failed because of their own irresponsible financial practices. Doing so, Paul and his libertarian colleagues asserted, was essentially the theft of resources from middle- and lower-class citizens to benefit wealthy, upper-class citizens. The libertarian position on failing companies ardently states that they should file for bankruptcy and be restructured so they can begin anew without unjustly absorbing funds from the American people.

The rest of the libertarian platform as it relates to the economy falls along similar lines. Libertarians oppose government involvement in all aspects of private American markets, from banks to the energy sector to health care. Libertarians believe that when government allows labor markets, the health care system, and the retirement-security market, for example, to operate freely among buyers and sellers, the entire American economy benefits. Libertarians firmly oppose all government aid to the poor, believing that charities and other nongovernmental organizations should instead rise to assist the less fortunate. Critics of libertarianism have accused the ideology of favoring the rich while dismissing the poor; the libertarian response is that with a vibrant and successful American economy, brought about by libertarian policies, the poor will be able to lift themselves out of poverty.

The following chapter presents multiple viewpoints relating to the libertarian view of the US economy. Topics covered include libertarians' stance on caring for the poor, libertarians' view on income taxes, and the libertarian idea of a basic income guarantee.

Viewpoint 1

"The libertarian position on the poor and poverty is clear, consistent, and uncompromising: It is not a legitimate purpose of government to provide antipoverty programs."

Libertarians Believe Government Has No Responsibility Toward the Poor

Laurence M. Vance

In the following viewpoint, Laurence M. Vance contends that although libertarians do not hate the poor, they sincerely believe it is not the government's job to provide welfare programs for them. Vance argues that a better American society would stop spending money on such initiatives and instead encourage the growth of charities so that the government could stop taking money from some to distribute to others. Vance is a columnist and policy advisor for the Future of Freedom Foundation.

Laurence M. Vance, "Do Libertarians Hate the Poor?," FFF.org, October 23, 2012.

As you read, consider the following questions:

1. According to Vance's research, how many Americans were living in poverty in 2011?
2. What percentage of federal income taxes does Vance say the top 50 percent of taxpayers pay?
3. What does Vance say is the only legitimate purpose of government?

The U.S. Census Bureau has released its annual poverty report based on the 2012 Annual Social and Economic Supplement (ASEC) of the Current Population Survey (CPS).

The CPS ASEC is a sample survey of approximately 100,000 households nationwide conducted over a three-month period in February, March, and April. The data reflect conditions in calendar year 2011.

The press release accompanying the publication of "Income, Poverty, and Health Insurance Coverage in the United States: 2011" reports that "in 2011, median household income declined, the poverty rate was not statistically different from the previous year and the percentage of people without health insurance coverage decreased."

According to the Census Bureau's press release, in 2011:

- The official poverty rate was 15.0 percent.
- There were 46.2 million people in poverty.
- 13.7 percent of people 18 to 64 (26.5 million) were in poverty, compared with 8.7 percent of people 65 and older (3.6 million) and 21.9 percent of children under 18 (16.1 million).
- After three consecutive years of increases, neither the official poverty rate nor the number of people in poverty was statistically different from the 2010 estimates.

- Real median household income in the United States in 2011 was $50,054, a 1.5 percent decline from the 2010 median and the second consecutive annual drop.
- Real median household income was 8.1 percent lower than in 2007, the year before the most recent recession, and was 8.9 percent lower than the median household income peak that occurred in 1999.
- Income inequality increased by 1.6 percent between 2010 and 2011.
- 6.2 percent of married-couple families, 31.2 percent of families with a female householder and 16.1 percent of families with a male householder lived in poverty.

The press release also noted that in the spring of 2012, 9.7 million young adults age 25–34 (23.6 percent) were additional adults in someone else's household.

The Political Economy

It is not surprising that Democrats and Republicans both tried to spin the numbers to their own advantage.

Rebecca M. Blank, the acting U.S. commerce secretary, issued a statement supporting the [Barack] Obama administration:

> It is clear that had President Obama not taken swift and aggressive action to grow our economy and create jobs, today's report would have shown much higher poverty rates, lower incomes, and a greater share of the population without health insurance. The Obama administration has also proposed a host of remedies that would help spur additional economic growth and job creation, but which are still awaiting congressional approval.

Speaking for the [Mitt] Romney campaign, Andrea Saul commented about the poverty report:

> Today's report confirms that the American Dream remains out of reach for too many families. Nearly 1 in 6 Americans

> are living in poverty, including a record number of women, and the middle class is struggling amid falling incomes, rising prices, and persistently high unemployment. While this may be the best President Obama can do, it's not the best America can do. Mitt Romney's pro-growth agenda will revive our economy, spur job creation, lift families out of poverty, and create a better future for our country.

The Democratic and Republican positions on poverty and the poor can be seen in their recently adopted party platforms.

In the Democratic platform, poverty is mentioned 15 times and the poor are mentioned 3 times. The Democratic Party believes it is the job of the federal government to "make ending poverty a national priority" and "help lift people" out of poverty, and specifically "people with disabilities" and "communities of color." To this end, it is committed to the Neighborhood Revitalization Initiative, the Sustainable Communities Initiative, growth zone initiatives, green-jobs training programs, community development, public and affordable housing, homelessness prevention, raising the minimum wage and indexing it to inflation, and refundable tax credits, the child tax credit, unemployment insurance benefits, and food stamps.

Democrats also think it is the business of the federal government to "reduce hunger and lift tens of millions of people from poverty across Africa." They will also invoke the poor to justify anything:

> "We understand that global climate change may disproportionately affect the poor, and we are committed to environmental justice."

In the Republican platform, poverty is mentioned six times and the poor are mentioned five times. The Republican Party likewise believes it is the job of the federal government to fight poverty. It is "committed to saving Medicare and Medicaid" because "absent reforms, these two programs are headed for bankruptcy that will endanger care for seniors and the poor." Medicaid should be "block-granted" to the states "with the flexibility to design programs that meet the needs of their low-income citizens." The Republican platform suggests that "such reforms could be achieved through premium supports or a refundable tax credit, allowing non-disabled adults and children to be moved into private health insurance of their choice." Public assistance "should be reformed to ensure that it promotes work." Programs "like food stamps must ensure that those benefits are better targeted to those who need help the most."

Republicans are as wedded to the welfare state as Democrats. Although they talk about limited government and fiscal conservatism in their platform and elsewhere, they are firmly committed to Medicaid, food stamps, unemployment, WIC [Women, Infants, and Children], SCHIP [State Children's Health Insurance Program], the earned income [tax] credit, housing assistance, and every other so-called anti-poverty measure. Welfare programs just need to be reformed, redesigned, or revamped.

The Libertarian Solution?

But what is it with the Libertarian Party? The only mention of the poor or poverty in their new platform is in this sentence: "The proper and most effective source of help for the poor is the voluntary efforts of private groups and individuals."

Do libertarians hate the poor?

First of all, government anti-poverty programs are doing a terrible job at alleviating poverty. According to Robert Rector, senior research fellow at the Heritage Foundation, "The federal government operates more than 80 means-tested welfare programs to provide cash, food, housing, medical care, and social services to poor and low-income people." Trillions of dollars have been spent on combating poverty since Lyndon

Johnson declared a war on poverty in 1964. "Welfare spending amounts to $9,040 per year for each lower-income American," remarks Rector. "If converted to cash and simply given to the recipients, this spending would be more than sufficient to bring the income of every lower-income American household to 200 percent of the federal poverty level."

Second, there are a lot of misconceptions about poverty in the United States. According to a Heritage Foundation analysis of the Census Bureau's poverty report,

- 80 percent of poor households have air-conditioning. In 1970, only 36 percent of the entire U.S. population enjoyed air-conditioning.
- 92 percent of poor households have a microwave.
- Nearly three-fourths have a car or truck, and 31 percent have two or more cars or trucks.
- Nearly two-thirds have cable or satellite TV.
- Two-thirds have at least one DVD player, and 70 percent have a VCR.
- Half have a personal computer, and one in seven have two or more computers.
- More than half of poor families with children have a video game system, such as an Xbox or PlayStation.
- 43 percent have Internet access.
- One-third have a wide-screen plasma or LCD TV.
- One-fourth have a digital video-recorder system, such as TiVo.
- 42 percent of poor households actually own their own homes.
- The average poor American has more living space than the typical non-poor person in Sweden, France, or the United Kingdom.

- 40 percent have an automatic dishwasher.
- More than half have a cell phone.

The scope and severity of poverty in the United States is certainly not what the raw numbers in the Census Bureau's poverty report lead us to believe.

Third, the poverty level figures are deceiving. According to the Census Bureau: "Currently, anyone earning less than $11,484 per year is considered to be living in poverty. For a family of four, the earnings threshold is $23,021 per year." However, that doesn't mean that individuals and families counted as making less than those amounts actually do so. Government assistance is *not* included when determining one's earnings. It is even stated by the Census Bureau: "The poverty estimates released today compare the official poverty thresholds to money income before taxes, not including the value of noncash benefits." A family of four "officially" earning less than $23,021 might be receiving $400 in food stamps every month and a $5,000 refundable earned income credit at the end of each year. That is the equivalent of almost $10,000 in additional income.

Fourth, the poor don't pay any federal income taxes. Although the Obama campaign and the Democrats in their platform talk about the "rich" paying their fair share, according to the IRS [Internal Revenue Service], the top 1 percent of taxpayers (in terms of adjusted gross income) paid 36.73 percent of all federal income taxes. The top 5 percent of taxpayers paid 58.66 percent. The top 10 percent of taxpayers paid 70.47. The top 25 percent of taxpayers paid 87.3 percent of the taxes, and the top 50 percent paid a whopping 97.75 percent. That doesn't mean that the poor should be forced to pay more; it just means that they don't have a federal income tax bill to pay.

Fifth, the Constitution nowhere authorizes the federal government to fight poverty. The powers delegated to the federal

© Adam Zyglis, "Rand Paul," The Cagle Post, April 13, 2015. All rights reserved.

government under Article I, Section 8, simply do not include the authority to set up anti-poverty programs or establish a safety net for Americans. But what about the "general welfare" clause in the Preamble and in Article I, Section 8, Paragraph 1? The clause says "general welfare," not "specific welfare" for certain individuals. It is neither the grant of a general legislative power to the federal government nor an additional grant of power beyond what is specifically enumerated in the Constitution. As the "Father of the Constitution," James Madison, explained,

> With respect to the two words "general welfare," I have always regarded them as qualified by the detail of powers connected with them. To take them in a literal and unlimited sense would be a metamorphosis of the Constitution into a character which there is a host of proofs was not contemplated by its creators. If the words obtained so readily a

> place in the "Articles of Confederation," and received so little notice in their admission into the present Constitution, and retained for so long a time a silent place in both, the fairest explanation is, that the words, in the alternative of meaning nothing or meaning everything, had the former meaning taken for granted.

And although the census itself is constitutional, the Census Bureau's poverty report is not.

Finally, and most important, fighting poverty is simply not a legitimate purpose of government. The only legitimate purpose of government is to protect the life, liberty, and property of its citizens from the violence or fraud of others. No matter how noble the intentions, government goes astray when it attempts to "help" or "fix" or "remedy" the plight of some person. Government has no resources of its own. The only way it can spend money to help one person is by taking it by force from another.

The Libertarian Misconception

The libertarian position on the poor and poverty is clear, consistent, and uncompromising: It is not a legitimate purpose of government to provide anti-poverty programs, safety nets, job training, welfare, income security, retirement security, medical care, premium supports, housing assistance, energy assistance, unemployment compensation, food stamps, or refundable tax credits.

That doesn't mean that libertarians hate the poor, are not bothered by malnourished children, don't care whether homeless people starve, or are not concerned about the plight of the poor.

It means that libertarians cherish the individual liberty, private property, personal responsibility, limited government, and free society that allow the actions of families, friends, philanthropists, humanitarian institutions, religious organizations, and charitable associations to flourish.

Viewpoint 2

> *"Are any taxes voluntary? Certainly not the income tax. . . . No, almost all tax schemes eventually involve some form of coercion."*

Libertarians Correctly Label Taxation as Coercive

Keith Farrell

In the following viewpoint, Keith Farrell argues that libertarians are correct in labeling taxes as a form of theft. He suggests various noncoercive alternatives for collecting funds from Americans, such as lotteries and sales taxes. Farrell advocates for these methods on the principle that forcibly taking money from citizens should not be the purpose of government. Farrell is a writer for the Libertarian Republic *newsmagazine.*

As you read, consider the following questions:

1. To what historical precedent does Farrell refer to support his suggestion of using lottery tickets to generate public funds?

Keith Farrell, "6 Ways to Fund Public Services in a Libertarian Republic," The LibertarianRepublic.com, September 22, 2013.

2. According to Farrell, what is an excise tax?
3. What does Farrell say would be the advantage of a voluntary tax in a community or town?

Are any taxes voluntary? Certainly not the income tax. Although Senator Harry Reid believes it is. No, almost all tax schemes eventually involve some form of coercion. As Mao Zedong said, "Political power grows out of the barrel of a gun" and there's nothing that gives a government more power than the laying and collection of taxes. But is there a way to collect taxes for public works without doing violence?

Every libertarian has heard the question: If not for coercive taxation, how would society ever maintain infrastructure and provide services? In other words, "Who would build the roads?"

Alternative Solutions

1. Lottery. Of course, in a libertarian republic, government would not hold a monopoly on lotteries, but nonetheless lotteries could be used to generate revenue through voluntary participation. Government could use a specific proportion of a lottery's revenue for funding and one or more lucky participants could win the rest. The Founding Fathers used this method. George Washington signed lottery tickets to raise money for public infrastructure.

2. Consumption Tax. A tax on spending on goods or services. A value added tax is a tax which is based on the value added to a product at each stage of production. For example, if a retailer were to buy a shirt for $5 and sell it for $10, the tax would apply to the $5 difference. Each stage of the production process would incur tax, leaving a final product with a price incorporating those taxes. A sales tax is simply a tax on the consumer at the point of purchase of goods or services. An excise tax applies to the sale of a specific good or

History of the US Income Tax

The origin of the income tax on individuals is generally cited as the passage of the 16th Amendment, passed by Congress on July 2, 1909, and ratified February 3, 1913; however, its history actually goes back even further. During the Civil War, Congress passed the Revenue Act of 1861, which included a tax on personal incomes to help pay war expenses. The tax was repealed ten years later. However, in 1894 Congress enacted a flat rate federal income tax, which was ruled unconstitutional the following year by the U.S. Supreme Court because it was a direct tax not apportioned according to the population of each state. The 16th Amendment, ratified in 1913, removed this objection by allowing the federal government to tax the income of individuals without regard to the population of each state.

Ellen Terrell, "History of the US Income Tax," Library of Congress, February 2004.

service by quantity—such as a per gallon gasoline tax. In each instance, the consumer is choosing to buy the good or service.

3. *Voluntary Tax*. In a community, town or city, a voluntary per person tax may be implemented. Services provided by the town such as fire and police services could only be utilized by persons who had paid the tax. Those who choose not to would be left to fend for themselves, hire private services or depend on volunteer services. With such a system, an introductory tax rate could be implemented and, with time, as more people joined, the cost per person would decline.

4. *Usage Fees*. Tolls on roads, parking meters, city water, sewage access and ambulance services which bill for usage are all current examples of people volunteering to use govern-

ment services or infrastructure for a fee. This is a much fairer way to generate the revenue needed to maintain and operate government infrastructure than one which taxes those who do not need or use those services. This model can be extended to trash removal and fire services.

5. Cooperatives. Instead of Social Security and Medicare taxes coming directly out of the pay of all Americans, those who wish to join together in a cooperative effort of investment or insurance purchasing would be free to, and those who didn't would be free to not participate. Group investment cooperatives could offer future planning for Americans. Competing cooperatives could offer high- and low-risk packages with differing returns. Group insurance packages could also be purchased by a cooperative, similar to the way in which employers now participate in group packages through private insurance companies.

6. Land Sale. Local, state and federal governments own a lot of land. Much of it is land that is not needed. Governments could sell this land or even hold a lottery for parcels of land or any unused government real estate. This revenue could be used to generate revenue for onetime projects, such as funding the building of a new road or courthouse.

Considering that in a Libertarian Republic the government would have a much more limited role, these are more than adequate means to generate revenue. A Libertarian Republic's government would provide national security, a justice system to protect people's rights, a civil law system to enforce contracts, and the provision of infrastructure for those means. Services and infrastructure beyond that would be provided privately whenever possible, if not left to localities and funded only through the methods above.

Viewpoint 3

"Libertarians are swindlers, who paint attractive portraits of freedom, which, however, have nothing to do with reality."

Libertarians' Anti-Tax Views Are Misguided

Benjamin Studebaker

In the following viewpoint, Benjamin Studebaker contends that the libertarian idea of taxation being theft is foolish and not practical. Inequality exists in all societies, he believes, and it would be perpetuated were it not for some form of government coercion, such as taxes. In this way, Studebaker claims, the taking from some to give to others is the only way to help the inherently disadvantaged. Studebaker hosts his own opinion blog on politics and the economy at BenjaminStudebaker.com.

As you read, consider the following questions:

1. Into what three components does Studebaker break down the libertarian argument against coercion?

Benjamin Studebaker, "Intellectual Hipsters: Libertarians," BenjaminStudebaker.com, November 16, 2012.

2. What metaphor does Studebaker use to describe libertarians who propagate rugged individualism?
3. To what other group of political philosophers does Studebaker compare libertarians?

There's another upstart group of intellectual hipsters in addition to the sceptics and the lovers of [Friedrich] Nietzsche—the libertarians. You've definitely met these hipsters before. They wax romantically about Ron Paul, some of them voted for Gary Johnson, they tend to like theorists like [Robert] Nozick and [John] Locke, and some of them are Ayn Rand–embracing objectivists. You know the type. Like all hipsters, their ideas are much less sophisticated and clever than they imagine, and their position is neither novel nor socially helpful. Of course, I cannot merely assert these things, I have to prove them. Let's go.

The Logic of Libertarianism

There are two central ideas in libertarianism:

1. Taxation is theft.
2. All coercion (except perhaps to protect property and prevent murder) is wrong.

How do they reach these positions? Here's a logical reconstruction of each:

Taxation is Theft:

1. People deserve everything they acquire justly (without stealing or killing people—through free and fair market interactions).
2. Theft is when someone takes something deserved away from someone else without consent.
3. Taxes take things people deserve away from them without their consent and are therefore theft.

Coercion is Wrong:

1. People have the right to do anything they want as long as it does not harm other people.
2. Only direct harm (theft, murder) counts as harm.
3. All other forms of coercion consequently violate people's rights and are therefore always wrong.

These are two very simple ideas, and that's why they appeal to so many people—libertarians imagine that those of us who do not accept these concepts are so thoroughly absorbed with our complex theories of justice that we have ignored the obvious. In reality, the obvious is not obvious, because the social sciences are not like the natural sciences. In the natural sciences, Occam's razor applies—the simplest solution is usually the correct one. Here, reverse Occam's razor applies—the simplest solution is almost *never* the correct one.

Why? Because both arguments are wrong from first principle:

1. It is extremely easy to challenge whether people deserve everything they acquire through market relations.
2. It is extremely easy to challenge the strict interpretation of harm.

You can argue that people do not deserve everything they acquire through market relations for any of these reasons and more:

1. Inheritance: the children of the poor have not done anything to deserve to be poor, yet their poverty reduces their economic opportunity.
2. Determinism: human behaviour is the product of genetics and socialisation and therefore the poor do not deserve to be miserable due to factors outside their control.

3. Utilitarianism: in the long run, everyone benefits from redistribution through Fordism [modern economic and social systems based on industrialized, standardized mass production and mass consumption] and Keynesian economics [the economic theories and programs ascribed to John M. Keynes and his followers].

Personally, I think all three are excellent objections, and I'm sure many of you have others.

You can argue against the strict interpretation of harm through many means as well:

1. A person's health choices can result in higher medical costs which must be borne by society via higher prices for insurance.
2. A person's economic choices can result in limited economic opportunity for other people or reduced economic utility for all.
3. A person's social choices can damage the well-being of family and friends.

All of these are reducible to the wider point, that human beings are, broadly speaking, quite interconnected to one another. Consider how many human beings, over how many generations, it has taken simply to permit you to read the words I'm writing, and you'll see what I mean.

The Interconnectedness Argument

The libertarians are flatly denying the existence of distributive justice and of communitarian or collective welfare. That's not "wise" or "clever," it's just small-minded and medieval. We may not like taxes, we may not like the government coercing us through law to behave in ways in which we would not choose, but, when our behaviour impacts other people (which it almost always does) and when we are benefiting from being part of a community, that produces obligations to obey just laws.

Why Has Inequality Grown?

Percentage who volunteered the following as the main reason why the gap between the rich and everyone else has increased.

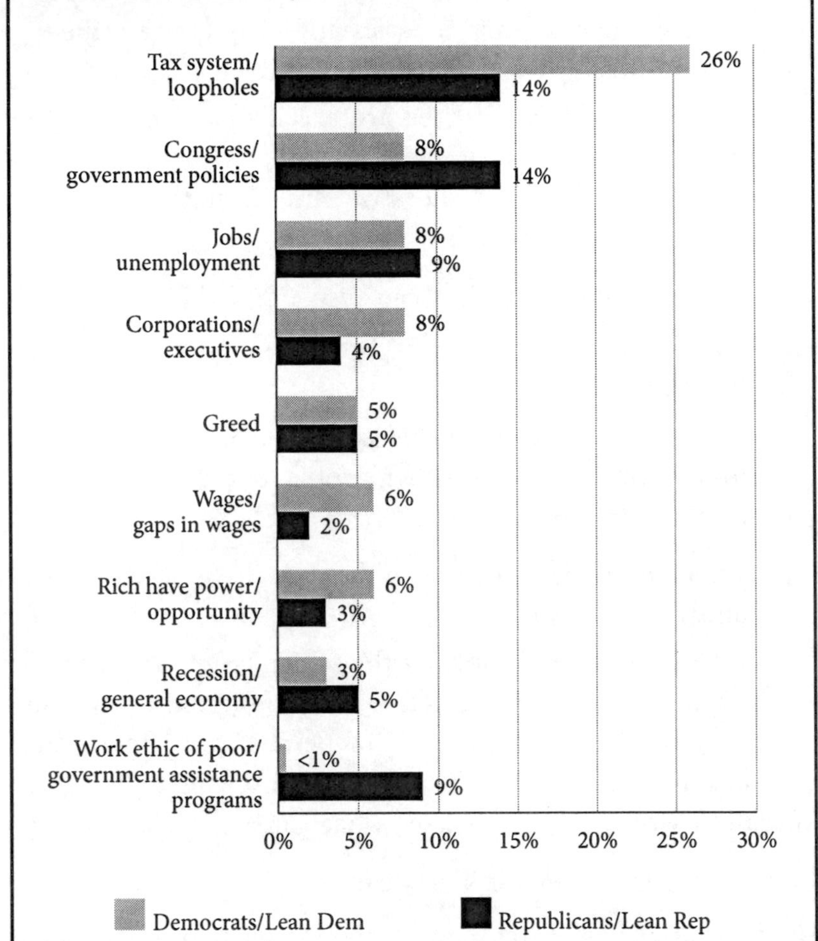

Source: Pew Research Center survey conducted Jan. 15–19, 2014.
Note: Question was asked of those who said there has been an increase between the rich and everyone else in the US in the last 10 years. Reasons are listed in order mentioned by entire sample that was asked the question.

TAKEN FROM: Drew DeSilver, "Americans Agree Inequality Has Grown, but Don't Agree on Why," Pew Research Center, April 28, 2014.

This is not to say that all laws and rules are just or that all should be obeyed—we still have to evaluate them for whether or not they are just—but it does mean that we cannot reject just laws on the basis of "I'm a free person, coercion and taxes are evil."

I would however offer to amend the punishment for violating laws for libertarians. Since libertarians are so thoroughly convinced that their actions do not have communal impacts, that they are entitled to everything they themselves produce, it is only sensible that, when libertarians break laws for libertarian reasons, we make their assumptions true for them. How would we make it such that libertarians had no impact on other people and were entitled to everything they produced? We would send them into the middle of the wilderness naked with absolutely no resources whatsoever completely alone and forbid anyone to contact them ever again. I would also suggest that we give them lobotomies that eliminate all knowledge they gained with the help of other people, but that sounds a bit cruel and unusual to me. If you want to be a rugged individual, be a rugged individual for real. Don't go around using arguments appealing to rugged individualism when you're more likely than not on a laptop, using the Internet, been educated by other people, been raised by parents, been taught a communal language, have the use of indoor plumbing, and so on down the line.

I would very much like to see what these libertarians could accomplish left to themselves with no resources, no language, no education, with no one to help them. I would compare them to the cavemen of ancient times and suggest that it would take them thousands of years to catch back up to where modern society presently is, but those cavemen have advantages that these rugged individuals would be denied—other people, communication, and the possibility of reproducing, for instance. The most likely outcome would probably be psychological breakdown followed by death.

So let me put the statist case very simply:

1. Everyone needs other people.
2. People naturally do not get along with each other perfectly.
3. We need taxes and rules to correct for the injustices that inherent incompatibility produces.
4. Taxes and rules need to be enforced to be effective, so we need to coerce people sometimes.

So the next time you meet a libertarian, don't be impressed. Don't allow yourself to be painted as a tyrant because you want a society in which cooperation is feasible and to everyone's benefit. A libertarian is an anarchist in a cheap suit. Libertarians are swindlers, who paint attractive portraits of freedom, which, however, have nothing to do with reality. They are the very picture of unrealistic idealists, in the same category as the hard-core Marxists [the political, economic, and social theories of Karl Marx]. Do not be fooled, do not be taken in, avoid the hipsters.

VIEWPOINT 4

> *"Libertarian support for basic income often comes through seeing it as the least bad way of dealing with poverty."*

Libertarians Rightly Support Basic Income for All

Jeremy Griffith

In the following viewpoint, Jeremy Griffith argues that the libertarian basic income guarantee would help end poverty in America. He cites research claiming that the guarantee would cost substantially less than the United States government's current welfare system. Additionally, Griffith contends, a basic income guarantee would allow recipients to feel more independent in spending their own money. Griffith is cofounder of the Unfettered Equality *blog.*

As you read, consider the following questions:

1. According to the viewpoint, why is the American welfare state demeaning to poor people?
2. How much would a basic income program allot to US adults each year, according to the viewpoint?

Jeremy Griffith, "The Libertarian Case for the Universal Basic Income," OpedSpace.com, January 28, 2015.

3. What does Griffith say is the heart of the challenge to basic income?

Basic income is a policy that would provide a uniform minimum income to all citizens of a nation. It is not a new idea, neither globally nor with libertarians specifically. Free market economist Milton Friedman supported a "Negative Income Tax," which eventually became expressed in an extremely watered-down way through the earned income tax credit (EITC). And [Friedrich] Hayek called for a "uniform minimum" back in 1944.

The Current System

Libertarian support for basic income often comes through seeing it as the least bad way of dealing with poverty than the current web of programs collectively referred to as the welfare state. Veronique de Rugy of George Mason University's Mercatus Center does of a good job of explaining this logic on *Reason*:

> "Welfare programs are demeaning by design, because they dictate to poor people what they must spend on food, housing, or health care, rather than letting them make those trade-offs themselves [...] The libertarian interest in a guaranteed income scheme proceeds not simply—or even mostly—from the desire to make government smaller and more cost-efficient. It stems from a belief that all individuals have the capacity to promote their own interests, and in fact are better able to make decisions about their lives than anyone else."

The current welfare state shoulders poor people with burdens of control and humiliation to go along with their financial hardships. Additionally, it is horribly inefficient. A Brookings Institution study found that the SNAP program [Supplemental Nutrition Assistance Program], for example, spends 15.8 cents on administrative costs for every dollar is-

Guaranteed Income in America?

The supporters of a guaranteed income are a varied lot. They range from unreconstructed communists to humanists with a strong sense of dignity and the wealthy. One concern that many of them share, however, is the global rise in income inequality. In the past few decades, economic growth lifted hundreds of millions out of poverty. But, at the same time, the distribution of income became increasingly skewed in favor of wealthy individuals. . . .

There are many reasons why income inequality has risen. One is technology, which tends to benefit the well educated. Machines increasingly take over routine tasks, leaving low-paid service jobs for unskilled workers. As a result, U.S. employment and wages tend to grow at the very bottom and at the very top of the distribution in skills. The middle is hollowed out.

Import competition from poorer countries is a second reason. Chinese imports, for example, explain about one quarter of the decline in U.S. manufacturing from 1990 to 2007. . . .

Beliefs about the reasons for poverty are critical for the willingness to redistribute income. People like to be generous if they think the poor are deserving of their support. But they have a strong aversion to giving if they suspect the less fortunate do not try hard to escape their circumstances.

Felix Oberholzer-Gee, "Will a Guaranteed Income Ever Come to America?," PBS NewsHour, *April 7, 2014.*

sued through food stamps—compared with 1.5 cents per dollar issued by the "Friedmanite" earned income tax credit.

Basic Income Obstacles

But of course the big question concerning basic income is cost. Charles Murray, author of the book-length call for basic income, *In Our Hands*, claims that a uniform minimum income of $10,000 per year could be provided to each adult US citizen 21 years of age and older for the same cost as the present welfare state. Additionally, he states that basic income would be far more immune to demographic shifts than our current system, noting that by 2028, his $10k-a-year option would end up costing a trillion dollars *less*.

But $10,000 a year is significantly below the current poverty line of $11,670. It is also bizarre—though mathematically convenient—that adults 18–21 are left out.

Furthermore, *Reason's* Veronique de Rugy is skeptical that it would be politically possible for basic income to fully replace the existing welfare state, stating that it would far more likely coexist alongside the existing tangled web of assistance programs, as "a new layer of spending on top of the old."

And this speaks to the heart of the challenge for basic income: for it to improve society, it would *need* to be accompanied by other societal changes as well. Certainly, for the reasons mentioned above, it should *replace* rather than supplement the existing welfare state. But more is required. Hayek put it well in 1944 in his *Road to Serfdom*:

"Let a uniform minimum be secured to everybody by all means, but let us admit at the same time that with this assurance of a basic minimum all claims for a privileged security of particular classes must lapse. . . ."

Hayek attacks here the *corporate welfare state*—the subsidies, privileges, and barriers to entry that Charles W. Johnson calls the "Invisible Fist" of state-sponsored poverty. For basic income to truly work, we would need to create a truly even playing field. Along with a "uniform minimum," we must also demand uniform *justice*.

It was Hayek himself, however, who stated in *The Fatal Conceit* that "evolution cannot be just," meaning that the wild growth of a free economy will never result in a distribution of wealth that is *morally acceptable*. There will always be winners and losers. There will always be those who are left in the cold *through no fault of their own*. Structural poverty. Structural unemployment. And structural racism. . . .

It's time that libertarians get comfortable with acknowledging and discussing structural inequality—and basic income gives us a way to do so without voicing support for a paternalistic welfare state. Progressives and libertarians should be able to see each other from across this narrowing divide, and my hope is that this policy debate becomes a turning point in the relationship between the two political camps.

VIEWPOINT 5

> *"I am unconvinced by the 'libertarian' arguments for forcefully taking money from some and giving it to others."*

Against "The Pragmatic Libertarian Case for the Basic Income Guarantee"

Ash Navabi

In the following viewpoint, Ash Navabi argues that the libertarian basic income guarantee would most likely be untenable in American society, as it requires taking money from some people and redistributing it to the poor. American capitalists who make millions of dollars, Navabi believes, will probably never agree to such a proposal. Instead, he writes, Americans should be gradually convinced to relinquish contributions voluntarily to help those in need. Navabi is a student at Ryerson University and a contributor to the blog of the Ludwig von Mises Institute of Canada.

Ash Navabi, "Against 'The Pragmatic Libertarian Case for the Basic Income Guarantee,'" Ludwig von Mises Institute of Canada (blog), August 15, 2014. https://mises.ca/posts/blog.

As you read, consider the following questions:

1. What are the four components of practicality into which Navabi deconstructs the libertarian call for basic income?
2. What characteristics does Navabi ascribe to a libertarian utopia?
3. To what famous principle does Navabi compare the libertarian nonaggression principle?

Self-styled "Bleeding Heart Libertarian" Matt Zwolinski is out with a new series of essays defending a "basic income guarantee" (BIG). For those who don't know, a BIG is a program where the government gives everyone, regardless of wealth or income, a set amount of cash every year. Professor Zwolinski has previously attempted to justify a BIG on philosophical libertarian grounds, which I considered unprincipled. He is now attempting to justify a BIG on "pragmatic" libertarian grounds. I have issues with this line of defense as well.

Zwolinski's argument for practicality boils down to four claims: that a BIG is cheaper than the current welfare state, a BIG is less paternalistic, a BIG would require a smaller bureaucracy, and a BIG would remove a lot of the opportunities for "rent-seeking" (meaning it would be harder for the rich and powerful to get special treatment). Zwolinski then attempts to brush aside principled libertarian arguments against a BIG by claiming that a libertarian "utopia is not an option".

Unfortunately, Zwolinski does not define what a libertarian utopia is, let alone argue why it is not an option. He merely states the fact that "most people are not libertarians." and many thinkers of the libertarian tradition (such Locke, Nozick, Friedman, and Hayek) have supported similar ideas to a BIG. But name-dropping is not an argument. So I'm going to do Zwolinski's work for him by defining a "libertarian utopia," and go on to defend why it is just as feasible an option as a BIG.

Following in the tradition of Murray Rothbard (who Zwolinski insinuated was a utopianist), I believe a libertarian utopia to a be a land where individuals have inalienable rights to their bodies, and can come to own property through either Lockean homesteading of unowned property or contracting with another person who has justly come to own that property. The initiation of force is unjustified, and private courts settle disputes.

That's it. Notice the things that are *not* part of this utopia: that there exists perfect harmony between all peoples, that no crime is ever committed, that the oceans are made of lemonade and roasted chickens fly straight into your mouth, that everyone is some sort of super genius, or that people are unthinking automatons.

A libertarian utopia (at least in the Rothbardian tradition) is strictly a world where individuals own themselves, can somehow come to own other things, and that aggressive violence against people and their properties is wrong (aka, the non-aggression principle/NAP).

Now, is this vision of utopia too far to reach from these earthly shores? Maybe. Again, as Zwolinski points out, most people aren't libertarian. But taken individually, all of the aspects described above of a libertarian utopia have earthly origins: the recognition of private property rights is thousands of years old, many have referred to the non-aggression principle as a variation of the "Golden Rule," variations of contracting and homesteading have been recognized throughout time and across many cultures, and there are numerous examples of private courts thriving.

But yet, most people today insist that libertarian utopia is untenable for various reasons: sometimes it's necessary to use violence to achieve some end, private courts are more likely to be corrupt, private property is exploitative, etc. This is an undeniable fact of today's political consciousness. And yes, it's true, as Zwolinski says, that there is no obvious way "to get

There"—a libertarian utopia—"from Here"—a world where most people can't imagine anyone but the government can build a road. But that doesn't mean people aren't trying to bridge this gap: between think tanks dedicated to reaching out to the general public, to think tanks more geared toward politicians, to university programs, to popular movements, and to literature & pop art, decentralized libertarian persuasion is gradually shifting the discussion and persuading more and more people. And evidence seems to suggest that, slowly but surely, it's working.

But as far as I can tell, Zwolinski is unmoved by this growth of libertarian thought among the masses. No, to Zwolinski these efforts are overzealous, and doomed for failure as they aim for an imaginary world where the systematic initiation of violence is not allowed.

But compare that world to Zwolinski's "pragmatic" libertarian vision: a world where the current patchwork of subsidies, bureaucrats, legal loopholes, and tax breaks is completely replaced by a BIG. And how we get to "There" from "Here," presumably (Zwolinski, despite chiding the utopianists earlier for this very problem, does not actually propose any sort of transition plan) is by millions of bureaucrats and crony capitalists (to say nothing of "welfare queens" and others who live largely or exclusively on the government's dime) enthusiastically agreeing to end their generous payouts of tens or hundreds of thousands, if not millions, of dollars of other people's money in favour of a BIG. (And it must be enthusiastic agreement, otherwise you would need a strong-armed libertarian government hell-bent on eliminating bureaucracy and cronyism, which won't happen because most voters aren't libertarians.) And they will do this because a BIG is more libertarian than the current system. . . . Even though, as Zwolinski himself pointed out, most of these people *are not libertarians!*

Now, gentle reader, which seems more "pragmatic": the method of decentralized persuasion, or the method of expecting oligarchs and lifelong bureaucrats to voluntarily give up their power? For me, slowly persuading more and more people of the feasibility and desirability of a voluntary society is more likely than to expect plutocrats to make moral decisions that harm them but benefit the poor.

So again, I am unconvinced by the "libertarian" arguments for forcefully taking money from some and giving it to others.

Periodical and Internet Sources Bibliography

The following articles have been selected to supplement the diverse views presented in this chapter.

Michael C. Bender and Peter Gosselin	"How Rand Paul Deviates from His Libertarian Dad on Economic Policy," Bloomberg, April 7, 2015.
Economist	"In Defence of Spontaneous Order," September 29, 2014.
Noah Gordon	"The Conservative Case for a Guaranteed Basic Income," *Atlantic*, August 6, 2014.
Damon Linker	"Libertarianism's Terrible, Horrible, No Good, Very Bad Idea," *The Week*, September 26, 2014.
Ian Millhiser	"Major Libertarian Thinker on Human 'Failures': 'It Is Best They Should Die,'" *Think-Progress*, April 15, 2015.
Marty Moore	"Economic Libertarianism Is Poppycock," *Sun-coast News* (Tampa, FL), May 19, 2015.
Lynn Stuart Parramore	"How Piketty's Bombshell Book Blows Up Libertarian Fantasies," AlterNet, April 28, 2014.
Noah Smith	"Austrian Economists, 9/11 Truthers and Brain Worms," BloombergView, July 2, 2014.
Doug Stuart	"Progressives, Libertarians, and God's Economy," LibertarianChristians.com, April 3, 2015.
Laurence M. Vance	"Libertarian Statism," LewRockwell.com, June 18, 2014.
Alan Wolfe	"Libertarianism's Iron Cage: From Ayn Rand to Rand Paul," *Commonweal*, September 15, 2015.

Chapter 3

What Is the Libertarian Stance on Social Issues?

Chapter Preface

Despite being considered an outgrowth of the Republican Party, American libertarians in fact hold a number of political positions that are fundamentally at odds both with their conservative base and the liberal leftism of the Democratic Party. As some commentators have asserted, libertarianism borrows stances from each party and combines them into a new set of principles meant to promote nearly unrestricted civil liberty for all Americans. Therefore, though each of the two major American political parties has located some common ground with libertarianism, the three political philosophies have remained different enough to continue opposing one another in most major elections across the country.

One area in which libertarians divert from Republicans is the matter of social issues. While the Republican Party adamantly opposes the nationwide legalization of same-sex marriage, abortion, and certain illicit drugs such as marijuana, most libertarians support these exact measures. This is not necessarily due to any sort of ideological agreement with liberal Democratic values, though some Democrats have supported libertarians for taking these positons in any case. Rather, the libertarian break from Republicanism on these issues stems from the core doctrine of libertarian thought: that individual liberties are broadened when the government is shrunk.

The Libertarian Party formed in 1971 as a movement to restore the United States to its early state under the Founding Fathers, when the federal government was heavily restricted from infringing on the personal freedoms of its citizens. One of the party's founding creeds called for the repeal of all laws against victimless crimes, as libertarians believed that outlawing any behavior that harmed no one was an example of government interfering in Americans' personal lives.

To this end, contemporary libertarians support the same social issues as Democrats, but for different reasons. The Libertarian Party, in its official political platform, notes that individual party members may personally support or oppose issues, such as abortion or gay marriage, despite the party's official advocacy for these issues, on behalf of unhindered civil rights. At the same time, however, libertarians themselves often disagree with one another over what the proper libertarian stance on an issue should be. Calling for the free exercise of certain civil liberties by one group of people, some libertarians claim, naturally entails infringing upon the freedom of another group. The question of which personal liberties eclipse others when advocating for various social issues has become pervasive among libertarians.

The following chapter presents viewpoints on libertarianism's relationship to various social issues affecting the United States. Subjects discussed include abortion, gay rights, and an open-borders immigration policy.

Viewpoint 1

> *"The right to life of the innocent child still trumps the temporary sacrifice of some of the mother's liberties."*

Libertarians Should Be Pro-Life

Kristen Hatten

In the following viewpoint, Kristen Hatten argues that a true libertarian would oppose abortion on the grounds that the government has no right to kill an innocent individual. Though a mother's liberty to control her own body is infringed upon by the pro-life position, Hatten admits, it is outweighed by the importance of saving the life of an unborn child. Hatten is the vice president of New Wave Feminists.

As you read, consider the following questions:

1. Of what three components does Hatten say the "night watchman" type of government consists?
2. On what belief does Hatten say libertarianism is firmly based?

Kristen Hatten, "Why Libertarians Should Be Pro-Life," LiveActionNews.org, September 9, 2013.

3. What does Hatten say is the problem with the relationship between the government and Planned Parenthood?

So guess what? I'm a libertarian.

I know, I know. Take a minute. It's gonna be okay.

I haven't always had the highest opinion of libertarians, so I'm willing to eat a little bit of crow. But only a little. After all, a lot of self-described libertarians are just begging for contempt by being more or less politically ignorant, but utterly convinced that war is always bad and pot is always good. Also, "end the Fed" for some reason! Ron Paul 2016! Wooo!

A Valuable Position

All that aside, the beginning of my own political and spiritual self-education began in 2006 when I became pro-life and thought, more or less: "Holy crap. If I was wrong about that, what else am I wrong about?" A humbling experience, to say the least, and one that forced me to look critically at virtually all my long-held beliefs.

It took another four years of seeking, study, discussion, and paying attention for me to finally accept—and admit—that I was no longer what we in America call a liberal, but a conservative. It was the ramming through of Obamacare [referring to the Patient Protection and Affordable Care Act] into law that put paid to [put to rest] the last lingering vestiges of my leftism.

But if we're lucky, we never stop learning. Although sometimes I wish I could. It's kind of exhausting, right?

I seem to be aligning more and more with those who advocate extreme curtailment of government, the idea being that government is a necessary—and perhaps inevitable—evil. Evil being the operative word.

Many writers, thinkers, and politicians, such as sci-fi legends Robert Heinlein and Neal Stephenson; fantasy legend

J.K. Rowling (the Harry Potter series, whether Rowling acknowledges it or not, is very libertarian); politicians Rand Paul, Ted Cruz, and in some cases Ron Paul; political philosophers like pro-life libertarian James A. Sadowsky, S.J.; and friends like writer/photographer Robert Jones have been valuable to me on this journey.

I can't point to one person, book, or idea that tipped my scale in favor of libertarianism. It has been a long and gradual personal path—maybe even a lifelong one. But I do think Randy England's little book *Free Is Beautiful: Why Catholics Should Be Libertarian* may have been the final straw. Having read about this political philosophy from many different angles, when England drew my attention to how it aligned with the Bible, the Catechism, and the teachings of many saints and popes, I realized the value of libertarianism with some finality, even while disagreeing with England on a few points. (Mainly foreign policy and defense—it's the one place where I tend to disagree with most, but not all, libertarians.)

The Justified View

I am morally aligned with Republicans on almost every social issue—pornography, gay marriage, prostitution, etc.—but find I have begun to disagree with the party establishment on the proper role of government when it comes to these things.

The so-called "social issue" which is the glaring exception to this rule is abortion. It is not a "victimless crime," as many argue prostitution, sodomy, and gambling are. All libertarians of all stripes—and in this I include objectivists, though they might, well, object—should oppose abortion. Anyone who advocates any kind of government, no matter how minimal, should support making abortion a criminal act.

How do I justify this? It's actually pretty simple.

If you advocate a small government, you must assign it limited goals. What are the most basic reasons for a government to exist? To keep people safe, from outside aggressors and from each other. Objectivism, for example, argues for a "night watchman" government: basically, the military, police, and courts. The military defends the people from outside aggressors, the police arrest and incarcerate criminals, and the courts decide guilt or innocence and hand down sentences, as well as settling civil legal disputes.

I mention the objectivist ideal to illustrate that even the most bare-bones government would have laws against citizens killing other citizens. Libertarianism, unlike objectivism, is based largely on the nonaggression principle, which says—to put it very simply—it is morally wrong to initiate aggression. Force is justified only when combating force.

Libertarianism is also firmly based on a belief in personal responsibility. If every man is and should be free to make his own decisions, it follows that every man must own the results of those decisions. Which is to say: If a man and woman have sex, they both accept the risk that a pregnancy might be the result, and accept the obligation to care for the resulting child.

Abortion seeks first and foremost to avoid responsibility. It also violates the nonaggression principle, for what is less an aggressor than an unborn human who came into being through no fault of her own, but due to the decisions of her parents?

The nonaggression principle also applies in cases of pregnancy due to rape, for again, the child had no say in her existence, and one act of aggression (abortion) cannot undo another (rape).

It's true that a woman sacrifices some liberties when she becomes—and stays—pregnant. But again—in the vast majority of cases, she knowingly and willingly had sexual intercourse, knowing a child might result. If she was too young and ignorant to know such a thing, or if she was raped, the right to life of the innocent child still trumps the temporary sacrifice of some of the mother's liberties.

Furthermore, the abortion industry is a statist, crony-corporatist construct if ever there was one. While its CEO [chief executive officer] makes six figures, "nonprofit" Planned Parenthood receives huge grants from the federal government. Where does the federal government get its money? From you and me. And we have no say in the matter. No matter your feelings on Planned Parenthood, the U.S. government is taking money from you and giving it to them, without consulting you about it. That is stealing, no matter how you slice it.

Of course, Planned Parenthood argues none of the federal funds are used for abortion. And I suppose we should take their word for it. I suppose we should also ignore the fact that the more money we give them for *not abortion*, the more of their own money they have to use for *abortion*. But this leap of logic is one Planned Parenthood's supporters seem reluctant to make.

A Fundamental Contradiction

I agree with libertarians that government must be severely limited to its most basic functions. But if government has any function at all, it should be protecting its most innocent citizens from the tyranny of abortion.

While some libertarians agree with me—Libertarians for Life argue eloquently against abortion—the contradictory Libertarian Party platform includes the following:

> We . . . hold that where governments exist, they must not violate the rights of any individual: namely, (1) the right to life—accordingly we support the prohibition of the initiation of physical force against others. . . .

And, a few paragraphs later, the following:

> Recognizing that abortion is a sensitive issue and that people can hold good-faith views on all sides, we believe that government should be kept out of the matter, leaving the question to each person for their conscientious consideration.

It's past time for the Libertarian Party—and all libertarians—to recognize that their official view of abortion makes no sense in relation to their principles and their stated belief in the right to life.

VIEWPOINT

> *"Abortions may be immoral, but they should not be illegal."*

Libertarians Should Be Pro-Choice, with Exceptions

Kevin Vallier

In the following viewpoint, Kevin Vallier contends that abortions are unfortunate and morally reprehensible but should not be illegal, as women own the rights to their bodies. However, to Vallier, the only circumstances under which abortion should be legal, from a libertarian perspective, is if a mother causes an abortion on her own, without outside assistance. Otherwise, this would be considered murder, Vallier believes. Vallier is a writer for the Bleeding Heart Libertarians *blog.*

As you read, consider the following questions:

1. According to Vallier, how does the doctrine of double effect apply to abortion?
2. What does Vallier say is a proportionately grave reason to permit an abortion morally?

Kevin Vallier, "The Prospects for a Pro-Life Libertarianism," BleedingHeart Libertarians.com, July 15, 2014.

3. Who does Vallier say pro-life advocates target instead of mothers who have abortions?

Imagine for the purposes of this [viewpoint] that personhood begins at conception, as many pro-lifers believe. Imagine further that you're a standard self-ownership libertarian, who believes that all people, fetuses and their mothers, have an absolute right of control over their bodies. What should abortion law be?

Standard Libertarianism Is Pro-Choice

The most common answer is to take a radically pro-choice stance: Because women own their bodies, they have an absolute right to do what they like with themselves, and as a result, they have a right to abortion. Some libertarians qualify this right by requiring that women give live birth to viable fetuses or at least to near-term fetuses, but the standard view, as I encounter it, is that while women may be morally required to give birth in late-stage pregnancy, they cannot be legally required to birth a child rather than having an abortion. After all, they own their bodies. So libertarian opinion tends to range from radically pro-choice to the more moderate viability-qualified pro-choice position I have described. The point is that the legality of abortion does not really depend on the personhood of the fetus for libertarians. Even if fetuses are persons, they're simply unfortunate enough to have mothers that prefer to kill them than compromise their bodily autonomy. Such abortions may be immoral, but they should not be illegal.

Prohibiting Third-Party Provision of Abortion?

I'd like to challenge this view. Perhaps other libertarians have advanced this line of reasoning in the past, but I've never run across it. While a self-ownership libertarian should probably hold that *pregnant women* have an absolute right over their bodies, libertarians can deny that women have the right to *contract with others* to help them with their abortions. The natural line of response is that if you have a right to your body, you have the right to voluntarily delegate that right to others. But I don't think that follows in this case. Remember: *no one* has the right to kill the fetus directly. The only reason a pregnant woman [can] have a right to an abortion is because she has a right to use her body as she pleases. She would have no right to kill a fetus outside of her own body. Thus, no third-party has the right to kill the fetus (again, assuming fetuses are always persons). In this case, the right of the fetus not to be killed trumps the right of the mother to delegate her right over her body to another person. So when a pregnant woman hires an abortion provider to kill her child (per assumption), she is essentially hiring a *hit man*, something libertarians are almost always opposed to.

So we end up with the unusual position that if fetuses are persons, then on standard libertarian views, pregnant women have an absolute (or viability-qualified) right to abortion, but they are not permitted to delegate that right to another person and no one else is permitted to take up that right.

The Life of the Mother and the Doctrine of Double Effect

A natural reply is to ask about the life of the mother. Surely if a mother's health is seriously endangered by the child inside of her, she has a right to delegate her abortion right to another person. I think that is right in this case, but only due to the activation of the doctrine of double effect [DDE]. Because the woman is not attempting to kill the child, but the child dies as an unintended, albeit foreseeable result of preserving her body, then the abortion is permissible even if the fetus is a person. And so hiring someone to help with the abortion should be similarly permissible.

But the DDE should only apply when the aim is preventing the mother from dying or enduring grave bodily harm. And this is because the conditions of the DDE aren't met in other cases. Here's the SEP's [Stanford Encyclopedia of Philosophy's] description of the conditions:

> A person may licitly perform an action that he foresees will produce a good effect and a bad effect provided that four conditions are verified at one and the same time: (1) that the action in itself from its very object be good or at least indifferent; (2) that the good effect and not the evil effect be intended; (3) that the good effect be not produced by means of the evil effect; (4) that there be a proportionately grave reason for permitting the evil effect.

When a medical procedure preserves the life of the mother, the action in itself is good. In this case, it is plausible that only the good effect (saving the mother) is intended, not the bad effect (the death of the child). The good effect is not produced by means of the evil effect (presumably saving the mother's life does not usually require killing the fetus first). And finally, there is a proportionately grave reason to permit the evil effect, as we must choose between the life of the mother (or preventing a grave harm to the mother) and the life of the fetus.

But in cases where the mother's life is not at risk, it is hard to see how abortion meets these conditions, unless you place so much weight on the value of the mother's ability to live freely for nine months that it overrides the value of a child being able to live its full lifetime. But while you might personally value autonomy that much, *libertarian theories of justice* cannot justify this valuing, and so cannot justify codifying it. Libertarians weight the right of all innocent persons to live equally, and if fetuses are persons, then they must be included. Highly valued autonomy for the mother cannot trump the right of the child against the third-party abortion provider.*

What Protection Agencies and the Minimal State May Do

So, suppose that fetuses are persons, what does this mean for a libertarian legal code? It means that either the minimal state or protective agencies are required to prohibit the provision of abortion by third parties but to permit abortions induced by the mother alone (perhaps with the viability qualification attached). This means that no mothers are punished for having an abortion, just the third-party providers.

And note that this is pretty much all pro-lifers want in the first place. Very few pro-lifers want to throw mothers into prison. Instead, they prefer to prosecute abortion doctors. If fetuses are persons, then I think standard libertarianism frequently requires their prosecution.

An objection: under market anarchism one must hire a protection service in order to have a right to have others protect you, and the fetus cannot hire its own protection service. So it may seem that the fetus has no right to have the protection agency stop its mother from hiring a third party and to prevent the third party from providing the service.

But here we can appeal to a libertarian account of children's rights where parents are the natural homesteaders of guardianship rights but can lose guardianship in cases of severe neglect. So children, as non-adult persons, cannot be owned, but the right to raise them can be owned. And those rights do not include the right to hurt the child. If the guardian wishes to hurt the child and makes plans to do so, then

* Assuming fetal personhood and self-ownership libertarianism, if a woman attempts to have an abortion and injures herself in the process, then others are permitted, and in many cases required, to help her improve her condition. But that is merely to stop the injury, and the medical aid must proceed in the most fetus-preserving way available.

she *forfeits* her guardianship rights, which can then be homesteaded by others, as guardianship has returned to the commons.

So long as the number of pro-lifers is high enough in a libertarian population, there will often be someone, somewhere prepared to homestead the guardianship rights lost by the abortion-attempting mother (perhaps the father, other family members or local churches), which would then ask their protective services to prevent the third party from providing the abortion. So even on a protection agency view, it looks like you can get the effect of a ban on abortion.

The Proper Way

In sum: *assuming fetuses are persons*, standard libertarianism should permit and perhaps require protection agencies and/or the minimal state to prohibit pregnant women from procuring third-party provided abortion services and to prevent third parties from offering that service, save in the case of the life of the mother. But it can neither prohibit the mother from causing an abortion on her own or punish her for doing so.

I'm not entirely confident in my reasoning here, so what do you all think?

(A very interesting question is what to do in cases where reasonable people disagree about whether fetuses are persons, which is our standard predicament. But that question will have to wait for another time.)

Viewpoint 3

"Most libertarians and libertarian organizations are great on gay rights."

Libertarians Rightly Support Gay Rights

Stephen Richer

In the following viewpoint, Stephen Richer contends that despite opinions to the contrary, American libertarians are historic proponents of gay rights. He states that libertarians believe individuals are free to make their own choices regarding their sexuality and that government should not base its treatment of people on their personal decisions. Richer is a law student at the University of Chicago.

As you read, consider the following questions:

1. According to Richer's research, which Supreme Court decision declared section 3 of the Defense of Marriage Act unconstitutional?
2. What percentage of American voters does Richer say identify as libertarian?

Stephen Richer, "No, the Libertarian Party Isn't Behind the Curve on Gay Rights," DailyCaller.com, January 6, 2014.

3. Which libertarian institution does Richer say advocated for gay marriage in two Supreme Court cases?

Tyler Lopez's new *Slate* article: "How Libertarians Failed Gay Rights" is awful.

But, nonetheless, the piece has stirred up quite the hornet's nest. The post has 683 comments, and it has prompted responses by Brian Doherty at *Reason*, Stephen Miller at the Independent Gay Forum, and "Libertarians Concerned" (in a long Dec. 30 [2013] Facebook posting). Perhaps the speedy and sizeable response is because we libertarians are an especially prickly bunch. Perhaps it's because we're well educated and like writing. Perhaps we had extra time to write because we didn't attend religious services during the holidays.

Whatever the reason, the libertarian spirit has also moved me, and so here are three reasons why Lopez's article missed the mark.

1. The Libertarian Party is very much on-the-record in support of gay rights.

From Lopez: *[T]he Libertarian Party website has no section devoted to LGBTQ [lesbian, gay, bisexual, transgender, questioning] issues. To find that content, users have to dig around in the site's archives. The results are laughably minor: The most recent press release mentioning "LGBT" came in 2010—all of it spent decrying President Barack Obama's "inaction" on the repeal of the Defense of Marriage Act and the U.S. military's Don't Ask, Don't Tell policy. LGBTQ Democrats are painted as victims suffering from the catchphrase "battered gay voter syndrome." Democrats, despite their recent efforts to expand gay rights, are labeled as oppressors. The cure for all this persecution is, of course, the Libertarian Party.*

The notion that omission equals disapproval wouldn't pass an LSAT logic class. By parallel reasoning, the GOP [Grand Old Party, referring to the Republican Party] doesn't care about gun rights: there is no gun rights section (see the GOP's issues page). Ditto, the Democrats on foreign policy (roll over the issues section) and you won't see anything mentioning foreign relations or foreign policy.

But we need not go down the logic route. Evidence of the Libertarian Party's support of gay rights is readily available. "Libertarians Concerned" writes: "[Lopez's] proof is that the home page for the LP fails to have a tab on gay rights. He didn't bother to look in the same tabs at the actual LP platform. It took me all of 2 seconds [to find material on gay rights]."

Lest you think that the author behind "Libertarians Concerned" has special researching skills, try searching: "Libertarian Party and gay rights." It will bring you to a page that most people are comfortable with—*Wikipedia*—which will tell you: "In 2013, the Libertarian Party applauded the U.S. Supreme Court's decision, *United States v. Windsor*, to strike down section 3 of the Defense of Marriage Act (DOMA) as unconstitutional. The Libertarian Party has supported same-sex marriage since its founding in 1971. . . . The Libertarian Party platform and Republican Party platforms are generally at odds of each other concerning LGBT rights."

The mentioned Libertarian Party platform is accessible on the Libertarian Party website, and a party's platform is usually its most credible pronunciation of its values. Section 1.0 of the platform (that's ONE—not exactly tucked away) reads:

> Individuals should be free to make choices for themselves and to accept responsibility for the consequences of the choices they make. No individual, group, or government may initiate force against any other individual, group, or government. Our support of an individual's right to make choices in life does not mean that we necessarily approve or disapprove of those choices.

Section 1.3 is titled "Personal Relationships" and reads:

> Sexual orientation, preference, gender, or gender identity should have no impact on the government's treatment of

> individuals, such as in current marriage, child custody, adoption, immigration or military service laws. Government does not have the authority to define, license or restrict personal relationships. Consenting adults should be free to choose their own sexual practices and personal relationships.

That sure seems like blatant support for marriage equality. As Austin Petersen comments at the *Libertarian Republic*: "[T]he party platform doesn't mince words when [it] talk[s] about personal liberties (1.0), and personal relationships."

Doherty's *Reason* article also mentions the prominence of gay rights on the party's platform, and Doherty includes other good bits of evidence demonstrating the Libertarian Party's support of gay rights. (In addition to the party's platform, 2012 Libertarian Party presidential candidate Gary Johnson—pro gay rights—is a good place to start a search).

2. Libertarians and libertarians are not the same.

I bet Lopez knows that not all libertarians (philosophy) are Libertarians (political party). But he's awfully casual about substituting one for the other. He begins by making the narrower argument that the political party isn't supportive of gay rights, but then he uses individual libertarians as points of evidence. 11 percent of American voters identify as libertarian, but only 1 percent of the country voted for the Libertarian Party in 2012. Clearly the overlap is far from complete, and the positions of one group should not be transposed to the other. If Lopez is interested in gaining a sense of the broader libertarian position on gay rights, then he would do well to look at groups like the Cato Institute, which filed briefs on behalf of gay marriage in both the *Windsor* case (DOMA) and the *Perry* case [*Hollingsworth v. Perry*] (Proposition 8), Students for Liberty (broadly supportive of gay equality), *Reason*, *The Skeptical Libertarian*, Libertarians Concerned, R Street Institute, *Volokh Conspiracy*, and so on. All of them are reliably supportive of gay rights.

Libertarians and Same-Sex Marriage

To get really basic, libertarians generally believe the power of government should be limited to what is necessary to protect the rights of the citizenry. There are a lot of different ways this belief manifests among libertarians and different libertarians draw the line in different places—there's as much variety of opinion among libertarians as there is among progressives and conservatives—but this is the underlying philosophy and it influences where a libertarian comes from. Freedom of association is one of these rights—the inherent right of human beings to choose with whom they want to spend their time and money, to unionize with, and to sell goods, services or labor to without unnecessary government intrusion.

It's important to understand then that libertarian support for same-sex marriage and civil liberties for gay people in general is not a result of how libertarians feel about gay people. It has nothing to do with whether an individual libertarian actually likes or is comfortable with being around gay people or even whether a libertarian thinks homosexuality is a natural outcome of biological diversity or whether gay people are going to hell. Support for same-sex marriage is a result of a belief that gay people, just like heterosexual people, have the right through freedom of association to create their own families and expect to be treated the same way under the law. Laws forbidding recognition of gay marriage are a government intrusion on this inherent right.

Scott Shackford,
"Libertarians, Gay Marriage, and Freedom of Association: A Primer," Reason, *August 19, 2014.*

Then there's the issue of the particular libertarian Lopez mentions: Walter Olson. Walter Olson, a libertarian obstacle to gay rights? Hardly. Using some top-notch, thirty-second-research skills again, I Googled, "Walter Olson gay rights." The first link that comes up is a BuzzFeed link titled, "Cato Scholar Hosting Benefit to Protect Maryland's New Marriage Equality Bill." The article details the powerful effort that Olson (who is gay) and many of his libertarian friends have made to support marriage equality in Maryland. The third Google link sends the searcher to a *Huffington Post* article Olson wrote in defense of gay parenting: "The New Campaign Against Gay Parenting." And the next link, a *Wall Street Journal* link, is to an article in which Olson begins: "For those of us who support same-sex marriage and also consider ourselves to be right of center, there were special reasons to take satisfaction in last Friday's vote in Albany. New York expanded its marriage law not under court order but after deliberation by elected lawmakers with the signature of an elected governor."

If Walter Olson is emblematic of libertarian opposition to gay rights, then Lopez needs to rethink his argument.

3. The Employment Non-Discrimination Act (ENDA)

Finally, Lopez makes the argument that the Libertarian Party (and libertarians?) are bad on gay rights because some don't support ENDA.

Rather than boldly argue for equal rights for everyone, Libertarians have merely argued for the dismantling of everyone's rights—the right to legal marriage, the right against workplace discrimination, and so on. That's not liberty; it's giving the green light to entrenched systemic discrimination. Libertarians could have led on this issue. Instead, they've fallen unforgivably far behind.

This is so wrong on so many levels. First, discrimination is when you treat certain groups as less equal. But, as Lopez acknowledges, libertarians want the law to treat gays and straights equally (just not in the big government sense that

Lopez wants). Second, why would libertarians take the lead on an issue that further impinges upon the rights of private businesses? That's a pretty key principle—that private actors and businesses should be able to do what they please so long as they don't violate the rights of others—of libertarianism. Third, since when did not being onboard with ENDA—one issue in the mainstream gay rights movement—make you non-supportive of the movement? Does all of Walter Olson's work for gay marriage, gay equality, gay adoption, and so on get nullified because he has a philosophical objection to government's involvement in private businesses? To use myself as an example for the first time in this [viewpoint], does the fact I mildly oppose ENDA for libertarian reasons make worthless the entire blog my friend and I created to move the Republican Party on gay rights (*The Purple Elephant*)?

As Lopez admits, libertarians and the Libertarian Party have historically been good on gay rights. And as even the slightest bit of research shows, most libertarians and libertarian organizations are great on gay rights, and the Libertarian Party is at least good on gay rights. In plain English, Lopez's argument is very, very weak.

Viewpoint 4

> *"For philosophical libertarians, the hard crux of the matter is that homosexual marriage erases more civil liberties than it protects."*

Libertarians Should Not Support Gay Rights

Anthony James Kidwell

In the following viewpoint, Anthony James Kidwell argues that supporting gay rights over other civil liberties is not a good position for libertarians to take. While libertarians believe they are supporting freedom by advocating for the legalization of same-sex marriage, Kidwell claims, they are actually infringing on the rights of religious people, for example, by making them accept such marriage as moral. Kidwell is a writer for DontComply .com.

As you read, consider the following questions:

1. What kind of approach does Kidwell claim libertarians support in regard to gay marriage?

Anthony James Kidwell, "Still Support Gay Marriage? How Un-Libertarian of You," DontComply.com, February 7, 2015.

2. How does Kidwell say churches have been threatened by the government in relation to gay rights?
3. What does Kidwell say is a better libertarian question to ask about American marriage?

Sexual freedom has long been a pillar of the libertarian philosophy. The idea that the state shouldn't interfere in private affairs, including marriage contracts, is hard to refute in light of how most government crusades shake out for the common citizen. But after the courts have championed the cause of marriage equality, many Americans are finding out just how revolutionary the concept is—and they're definitely not feeling the love.

Not surprisingly, social liberals are applauding the left-leaning courts of late, for striking down traditional definitions of marriage at an alarming rate. For all the precedent in human history validating the purpose of marriage as the foundation of the natural nuclear family, in only the last decade, most of the country including the federal government and the District of Columbia have either come out of the closet—or have been forced out.

Today [in February 2015], 36 states recognize same-sex marriage. As the Christian-based Family Research Council points out, all but three of these radical shifts in the definition of society's most basic structure are the result of unaccountable, unelected and almost insurmountably permanent court decisions. To a libertarian, this should present a major problem.

Court Radicalism

Libertarians, both as a philosophical subset and as a political party, advance a cause of equality, including a *laissez-faire* approach to homosexuality and homosexual marriage, with a view that the state's place is neither to discriminate against nor legitimize contractual unions between individuals. Under the rule of the courts, however, the ideal of equality that libertarians hold dear has been twisted into a nightmare rarely ever seen this side of the Iron Curtain [a barrier formerly isolating an area under Soviet control].

Under the rule of the legislating judiciary, it's not at all *laissez-faire* for many Americans. On the contrary, this radicalism on the part of the courts has real, harmful consequences regarding our understanding of the First Amendment. The second-order effect of creating a new right to a state-recognized homosexual marriage is that your freedom of religion is immediately abridged. Especially so, should you dare take your religion out of church and into the workplace—for as it now stands, there is absolutely no legal protection for your conscience.

Aaron and Melissa Klein, owners of Sweet Cakes by Melissa, learned this the hard way, as they were just this week handed a livelihood-crushing $150,000 fine from the state of Oregon, which may be adjusted up to as much as $200,000 pending a March 10 hearing, for politely refusing to bake a cake for a gay wedding ceremony. The reason for their refusal? Aaron and Melissa are Christians and feel that participating in a homosexual ceremony would violate their deeply held religious beliefs. Because they dared to let their conscience guide their business practices, their mom & pop wedding business has been effectively stamped out by a gleefully coercive state, and they will be forced to surrender what probably amounts to four or more years of labor, all for having the audacity to hold a belief and act upon it.

They're not alone either. In states that recognize homosexual marriage, Christians in the wedding service industry from photographers to bakers to wedding planners are being forced out of the workplace for not participating in the radical redefinition of marriage, and the wholesale persecution is just beginning.

The Libertarian Case for Traditional Marriage

One of the great calumnies against the libertarian movement is that it is anarchistic in nature, proselytizing for a world without any kind of governing system to restrain the will of the individual. This libel can be traced all the way back to Thomas Hobbes, who erected the straw man of a world without Leviathan in which life is "solitary, poor, nasty, brutish, and short." From then until the present day, the defenders of limited government and personal liberty have contended with an opposing narrative of a nightmarish "libertarian" world, replete with stock characters such as the robber baron and the Somali warlord. . . .

Presently, our society is facing an unprecedented, albeit long in the works, threat to the strength and integrity of the family. Many libertarians have been sadly duped into fighting on the wrong side of the battle. As previously stated, there are many ways in which man organizes himself in a free society. . . . What defines his family, though, rests on our traditional understanding of marriage: one man and one woman coming together in a lifelong commitment out of which children may naturally arise. . . .

As a movement, libertarians must stand shoulder to shoulder in defending the last best hope that civil society possesses in resisting the onslaught of Leviathan. The movement must not succumb to the leveling impulses of the statists who would see marriage defined down and outward until said definition was so broad as to be rendered meaningless.

Mike Gannon, "The Libertarian Case for Traditional Marriage," Pocket Full of Liberty, *June 4, 2013.*

Even the church itself is threatened, as we have seen in Houston this past year when openly homosexual mayor Annise Parker attempted to subpoena the sermons of several pastors, to be scanned for defenses of traditional marriage that contradicted her idea of "equality." Parker's intent was to use the Houston churches' tax-exempt status to intimidate those pastors into silence. She would have succeeded in this blatant abuse, but for the loud public outcry that eventually forced her back into her place.

Totalitarian Libertarianism

All told, when one honestly looks at what's being done in the name of equality, supporting gay marriage turns out not to be very libertarian after all, but is actually very totalitarian when put to practice. The homosexual agenda turns out not to be about liberty, but instead is revealed to be just one more way for the state to control you and circumvent your rights.

For philosophical libertarians, the hard crux of the matter is that homosexual marriage erases more civil liberties than it protects. Or more properly stated, it erases "inalienable rights," such as the right to participate in the workforce without compromising your religious values, and replaces them with a false substitute: "civil liberties."

Here we find yet another fatal flaw in allowing government to administer justice. Despite all the left's rhetoric about liberty and equality, the homosexual agenda through gay marriage is being used as a blunt weapon against Christians, especially those who choose to do business based on their deeply held values. It's also being used to undermine the rule of law and the democratic process itself. Defining marriage between a man and woman is overwhelmingly supported by voters, yet it's a handful of activist judges who take it upon themselves to override those votes.

Protecting someone's choice to engage in certain behaviors, and forcing others to affirm and support those behaviors against their will, are two dangerously different things. Proponents of gay marriage should not get away with packaging that abuse in any way that casts it in a light of fairness and equality, and libertarians who believe in true equality should take them to task about the deception.

Instead, let us propose an alternative view. It would be a far more "libertarian" question to ask why all marriage is illegal by default—that is, until we pay the state for a "license" to wed. And why do church clergy at religious ceremonies, despite being protected from the iron fist of government by that ever-elusive wall of separation, still invoke "the power vested in me by the state of . . . ?"

Until those fundamental questions are resolved, it doesn't matter if we argue for or against same-sex unions. It doesn't matter if the Supreme Court upholds the several states' right to define marriage based on the will and consent of their citizens. Until we figure out exactly what a marriage is, and where the authority to wed and have children comes from, both paths inevitably lead us to subjugation.

Viewpoint 5

"Open borders is not a rational policy, even for a free, laissez-faire country."

Libertarians Wrongly Support Open Borders

Nelson Hultberg

In the following viewpoint, Nelson Hultberg contends that libertarian support for an open-borders immigration policy is wrong for the United States. Although some immigration is acceptable to Hultberg, he believes that an unrestricted influx of immigrants into America would breed a chaotic multiculturalism of the type that has afflicted many violent areas of Europe. Instead, Hultberg argues for a crackdown on illegal immigrants to save the cultural integrity of the United States. Hultberg is director of Americans for a Free Republic and the author of The Golden Mean: Libertarian Politics, Conservative Values.

As you read, consider the following questions:

1. What part of American culture does Hultberg say a correct immigration policy will protect?

Nelson Hultberg, "Where Libertarians Go Wrong on Immigration," CanadaFreePress.com, October 28, 2013.

2. What does Hultberg say prevents the creation of a world without nations?
3. Which ethnic groups does Hultberg say will make up the majority of the American voting bloc in fifty to one hundred years if present immigration trends continue?

Libertarians and conservatives agree on many issues and are allies in the fight against statism. But there are several areas where they disagree quite vehemently. One of them is immigration.

The libertarian refrain goes something like this: Isn't a policy of "open borders" the only approach consistent with freedom and individual rights? Besides, policing the borders and restricting immigration requires still another government bureaucracy. And for pete's sake, we have enough of those already.

The conservative answers that capturing criminals, defending the nation, and engaging in foreign relations require bureaucracies also. But they are necessary bureaucracies. Immigration policy is no different. It is a legitimate function of our government—to defend the borders and preserve the freedom and order of society.

The question is not, should we as a nation allow for "open borders," or endeavor to "close down our borders." The question is, what level of immigration is conducive to preserving the American culture of *ordered liberty?* Closed borders (permanently) would asphyxiate us; open borders would balkanize us. Ever since the 1965 immigration act, we have been hell-bent to balkanize ourselves. With the stratospheric rise in illegal immigration over the past 30 years, the balkanization process is now firmly imbedded in our culture and spreading its ruin at an accelerating pace.

Yes, America has always been a nation of immigrants. But never has she been a nation of *unrestricted* immigration. From the beginning of their formation of America into a nation, the founders were acutely aware of the need to lay down rules for entrance into the country and the acquiring of citizenship.

The Founders' View

The founders realized that the eternal verities such as our basic individual rights do not change from the past to the future, but immigration rules are not eternal verities; and basically they have nothing to do with the issue of individual rights. They are matters of public policy that will always be subject to both quantitative and qualitative revision with the passage of time.

In other words, entrance into a country is not a "right." It is a "privilege" granted by the citizens of the country involved. If those citizens decide their country would be better off with a small, selective stream of immigrants instead of a large and indiscriminate stream, then it is their right to bring about such a border policy. There is no such thing as a right to enter any country one chooses, no more than there is a right to trespass on the personal property of one's neighbor, or enter his house uninvited.

As the Supreme Court rightly ruled in the latter 19th century, "It is an accepted maxim of international law, that every sovereign nation has the power, as inherent in sovereignty, and essential to self-preservation, to forbid the entrance of foreigners within its dominions, or to admit them only in such cases and upon such conditions as it may see fit to prescribe."

The founders certainly agreed with this. George Washington told his contemporaries that, "The bosom of America is open to receive not only the opulent and respectable stranger, but the oppressed and persecuted . . . if by decency and propriety of conduct they appear to merit the enjoyment." . . .

Since the same principles and concerns that built America are needed to sustain her, we in the modern day too must be concerned with both the quality and the quantity of immigrants that enter the country. With the world's and the country's populations increasing relentlessly, America hardly needs to be adding millions of newcomers from outside our borders. Our population is growing steadily on its own.

Thus if our nation can be said to possess a culture or a certain "way of life," then any immigration policy we adopt must be geared toward preserving that way of life. Reason demonstrates quite clearly that unlimited, indiscriminate immigration is a dire threat to our way of life.

The Libertarian Flaw: Bad Ideology

Unfortunately libertarians cannot properly confront this dire threat because the great bulk of them believe in "open borders" for all nations. They don't believe in the nation-state concept as it has evolved over the centuries. They want to form a borderless world where all humans are allowed to migrate wherever they wish. The anarcho-capitalist libertarians want to do away with all government itself. Thus in any public debate over illegal immigration, libertarians self-destruct in the public's eyes. They come off as blind utopians divorced from reality who would destroy America and her political principle of "federalism," which is the only way to make freedom work in the real world. I discuss this problem of libertarianism extensively in my book, *The Golden Mean: Libertarian Politics, Conservative Values.*

There will never be a world without nations because there will never be a world without human nature, which is very concerned with ethnicity. It is born into us. To try and legislate humans into apathy about ethnicity is like trying to breed tigers into turtles. Reality does not allow such nonsense. Ethnic solidarity is one of the major reasons why nations come into being. Humans wish to gather among their own ethnic kind.

This, of course, doesn't mean that a nation must be all one ethnic group. But it must remain primarily its original (or dominant) ethnic group. Multiculturalism was one of the primary reasons for the fall of Rome. It has wreaked savagery and chaotic cruelty throughout the modern-day Balkan states. It is lethal to the maintenance of a free and stable society. This is why conservatives espouse "ordered freedom." Freedom cannot exist devoid of tradition and slow, minimal immigration.

Tossing Freedom in the Trash

The first step toward getting on the right side of this polarizing controversy is to grasp that all nations possess cultures that are delicate sociological balances of long-standing traditions, mores, and metaphysical views. In nations that lean toward freedom, their cultures are especially dependent upon these balances not being upset in a sudden and irresponsible fashion. Freedom is like an orchid. It is fragile and prone to being tossed in the trash by obtuse mobocracies that have not been taught to value it.

The illegals streaming into our country today have no grasp as to what freedom and its requisites are. To make matters worse, many of them are brazenly anti-American with an arrogant sense of entitlement already built into their personalities. They are bringing with them the political and cultural assumptions of their country of origin. And those assumptions are that the state is meant to take care of them. Unlike earlier America, we now have a state that will cater to those assumptions. This is the flaw in the rationale of open-border advocates. *The quality of immigrants that flows to a welfare state country will not be the same as that which flows to a laissez-faire country*. For this reason alone, any influx of immigrants to our nation must be severely restricted.

But as the founders knew, even in a laissez-faire country immigration must always be restricted. Today's unbridled welfare state merely makes restriction all the more mandatory. In fact it makes restriction a matter of national survival.

The flippant libertarian retort to this dilemma, that "all we need to do then is just get rid of the welfare state," is naïve and irresponsible. Open borders is not a rational policy even for a free, laissez-faire country. Moreover, the welfare state will require 50–100 years to phase out. If present immigration trends continue, in a half-century Mexicans and Central Americans (and their socialist assumptions) will have overrun the entire Southwest and much of the Midwest. They will be the majority voting bloc in the country. Thus all libertarians do with their flippant advocacy is confuse the populace, which allows collectivist bureaucrats and corporatists to continue bringing in larger and larger swarms of illegals. Rationality is needed here, not flippancy.

Here lies our danger. Because of Republican greed for cheap labor and Democratic greed for new party members, Washington is opening up the nation's doors to millions of legal and illegal immigrants from third world cultures who have no respect for [Thomas] Jefferson's "regime principles" of individualism, self-reliance, and equal rights under the law. To compound the problem, our welfare state schools are teaching all today's immigrants the precise opposite of these Jeffersonian principles.

The vision of America launched by the founding fathers is flagrantly smeared throughout our schools today. Our textbooks openly denigrate the founders as "aristocrats" and "elitists," and depict Western civilization and capitalism as evil, exploitative, racist, and criminal. Our professors teach that the country must be transformed into a collectivist society. Success, security, and health are no longer personal responsibilities; they are to be granted to us by the all-powerful state via massive redistribution of earnings.

It therefore comes as no surprise that millions of immigrants now swarming into America view themselves as right-

Open Borders: A Threat to Public Health

The [Barack] Obama administration's unrelenting focus on open borders has exposed Americans to deadly diseases and has politicized the public health agencies that are charged with protecting the health of Americans—the Centers for Disease Control [and Prevention] (CDC), the National Institutes of Health (NIH), the Department of Health and Human Services (HHS), and the Department of Homeland Security (DHS).

Rather than putting the health of Americans first, these agencies, which once took their roles to protect the public seriously, now go to great lengths to ensure that foreign nationals from countries with serious diseases are allowed to freely enter the United States. . . .

The CDC, NIH, and their fellow travelers use the same arguments to justify allowing individuals from Ebola areas into the United States as other open-border advocates do to justify a never-ending flow of illegal immigrants:

- The borders cannot be controlled so we have to let everyone in.
- We can't ask foreign nationals to respect American sovereignty and American immigration laws, otherwise they will just lie to get around them. . . .

At one time, the role of the federal government was to protect American citizens by controlling the nation's borders and protecting its citizens from public health hazards. Now it seems that the federal government is more interested in pursuing an open-borders policy regardless of the dangers that this poses to its citizens.

Ronald W. Mortensen, "Open Borders: A Threat to Public Health," Center for Immigration Studies, October 28, 2014.

ful recipients of an ever-increasing array of privileges, quotas, subsidies, and handouts. Incredibly this view extends even to the illegals.

The Demopublicans' Default

Naturally establishment politicians have constructed appropriate spin to avoid facing this pink elephant that sits in their ideological living room stinking up the future of our country. But none of the objections from the liberal multiculturalists and the conservative corporatists hold water in face of what should be our ultimate concern—the preservation of a sovereign America with our distinctly American culture of *ordered freedom under the dictates of objective law.*

Our solons on the Potomac are selling out our birthright to the globalists in pursuit of regional government and the end of American sovereignty. It is the most craven and shortsighted sell out in our history. Both Republicans and Democrats are obsessed with the illusions of multiculturalism. Both are poisoned with altruistic guilt concerning the poverty of the third world. Both are blind to the balkanization morass into which they are driving America.

Despicable indeed. But a nation gets the politicians it deserves, and we have reaped an assortment of quislings that now slither around in the most fetid of Machiavellian muck.

Our stand as patriots must be a restoration of the pre-1965 immigration accords and a return to a far more selective process in the qualitative requisites needed to enter the country. In addition, we must steadfastly insist on legislation that 1) mandates English as the official language of America, 2) closes the anchor baby loophole, 3) denies welfare services to illegals, 4) enacts E-Verify [an Internet-based system that allows businesses to determine the eligibility of their employees to work in the United States], and 5) prosecutes the present laws on the books about hiring illegals.

Will E-Verify threaten us with a national ID? No more than we already have with our Social Security number. E-Verify merely opens up the database to all private employers so they can easily verify an applicant's citizenship.

The above five policies remove the attractiveness of illegally entering the country. If we do not remove the lures that bring the illegals here, they will continue coming. For soft and squeamish Americans, such policies will seem cruel. For tough-minded patriots, they are just and necessary if we are to save the country.

Libertarians among the freedom movement will have to reexamine their policy of "open borders." It is not a policy that any rational American can afford to adopt. The founders' wisdom and the vast experience of mankind over the millennia must become the basis of our policy again on the vital issue of immigration.

VIEWPOINT 6

> *"The last remaining barrier to economic liberty is the free movement of people."*

True Libertarians Support Open Borders

Chris Berg

In the following viewpoint, Chris Berg argues for the free movement of people through the open borders of all nations as part of worldwide economic liberty. People should be free to relocate anywhere they want, Berg contends, if it means creating better, more prosperous lives for themselves. Any crackdown on a country's immigration policy, Berg believes, is a step away from true liberty. Berg is policy director at the Institute of Public Affairs in Melbourne, Australia.

As you read, consider the following questions:

1. According to Berg, what does conservative politician David Brat claim are three problems created for Americans by illegal immigration?
2. What does Berg say have been the victories of free markets over several decades?

Chris Berg, "True Economic Liberty Means More Open Borders," Abc.net.au, June 16, 2014.

3. What objection does Berg say the conservative right raises concerning illegal immigration and welfare?

There are two versions of David Brat, the upstart who defeated House Majority Leader Eric Cantor in the Virginia Republican primary last week [in June 2014].

The first is a professor of economics at Randolph-Macon College in Virginia—a principled libertarian, dedicated to the cause of economic freedom.

Brat describes himself "a free-market guy," who believes the economy has been badly distorted by regulation. He runs something called the BB&T Program on Capitalism, Markets and Morality. He's passionately opposed to the mass surveillance program exposed by Edward Snowden. His academic research focuses on the intersection between Christian theology and the market economy.

That's the first version of Brat.

The second version is different—an anti-immigration warrior for the conservative right. He ran hard against Cantor on the latter's support for amnesty for the children of illegal migrants.

In this campaign, Brat argued immigration "lowers wages, adds to unemployment, and the taxpayer pays the tab for any benefits to folks coming in." (Just as the asylum seeker debate is in Australia, the question of amnesty for illegals is a proxy for the broader question about how open the United States should be to immigration.)

For these sentiments he received endorsements from conservative firebrands like Ann Coulter—Brat was a candidate "true patriots should support with everything they have"—and Laura Ingraham.

Freedom and Open Borders

It's not easy to bridge the divide between the two Brats. There's nothing "libertarian" or "free market" about an immigration crackdown. Quite the opposite.

The great free market victories over the last few decades have meant goods and capital can move around the world freely. This has raised living standards for everyone, rich and poor.

The last remaining barrier to economic liberty is the free movement of people.

It's as much a barrier of political philosophy as it is a barrier of legislation. As Brat demonstrates, even some of the most hard-core free market advocates have a blind spot when it comes to immigration.

Yet what could be more respectful of the tenets of individual liberty than allowing individuals and families to travel across national borders to make a better life for themselves?

And what could be more inconsistent than claiming to believe in the morality of liberty but then placing the strictest of possible limits on that liberty?

On *The Drum* in 2011 I argued that to prevent migration is to prevent the most powerful way to lift people out of poverty. Migration is a big deal economically too. Opening the world's borders could double the size of the world's economy, according to one famous estimate.

Yet one of the doyens of free market thought, the Nobel-winning economist James Buchanan, said the hardest essay he ever had to write was on whether governments could justifiably restrict immigration.

There are two objections to larger scale immigration that you commonly hear from the intellectual right. Neither are strong.

The first is that increased immigration is incompatible with the welfare state. In this view, allowing large-scale migration is great in theory, but we have generous welfare programs. There's a risk some immigrants might migrate with the goal of hopping on Social Security. This argument was made by no less an authority than Milton Friedman.

But it's almost comically easy to resolve the apparent incompatibility: cordon off welfare programs to new migrants for a certain amount of time. In fact, that's exactly what we do in Australia (with the exception of refugees, who constitute a small fraction of the total migration intake).

The second objection is migrants may not assimilate to the national culture. This is not helped by the fact that many of the loudest pro-immigration voices are on the left and espouse a woolly sort of multicultural utopianism. But the point of a liberal framework of laws is that people of different values, preferences and beliefs can go about their business while everybody's rights are equally protected.

And let's not overestimate the cultural consensus among those born in the developed world. In Australia, the Lowy Institute [for International Policy] poll has been recording remarkably low support for basic things like democracy for many years.

Yet somehow the commonwealth endures. As it would with a larger—even vastly larger—immigration intake.

(If your concern is that immigrants might vote for illiberal policies—that is, undermine the liberal legal framework—note that immigration and citizenship are different things.)

Let's be clear—Brat is more philosophically coherent than 99 per cent of the politicians out there. Any defeat of an established Washington politician is a win. In response to Brat's attack on immigration, Cantor surged hard to the right on amnesty. Self-interest beats principle.

And even taking Brat's views on amnesty into account, American politics will be better off with him in Congress rather than a Beltway native like Cantor.

Brat ought to be praised for his scholarship on the connection between morality and free markets.

But it's also time for politicians who proclaim the virtues of liberty to discover its connection with the free movement of people.

Periodical and Internet Sources Bibliography

The following articles have been selected to supplement the diverse views presented in this chapter.

Jonathan H. Adler	"What Does It Take to Convince Libertarians and Conservatives That Climate Change Is a Problem?," *Washington Post*, April 14, 2015.
David Bier	"Libertarians Should Care About America's Ban on Immigration," Foundation for Economic Education, May 21, 2015.
Richard A. Epstein	"The Libertarian: Discrimination, Religious Liberty and How We Undervalue Free Association," *Federalist*, April 2, 2015.
Doug Hill	"Beware the Silicon Valley Elite: Ayn Rand, Google Libertarianism and Indiana's 'Religious Freedom,'" *Salon*, April 6, 2015.
Patrick O'Connor	"Libertarian Group Aims to Influence Immigration, Climate-Change Policies," *Wall Street Journal*, January 29, 2015.
Andrew Pearson	"There Is No Libertarian Argument Against Immigration," European Students for Liberty, December 23, 2014.
Sheldon Richman	"No Solid Libertarian Argument Against Legalizing Same-Sex Marriage," Reason.com, June 28, 2015.
Ben Shapiro	"Fake Libertarians Run from Religious Freedom Restoration Act," Breitbart, April 2, 2015.
Jacob Sullum	"Can Rand Paul's Positions on Abortion and Gay Marriage Be Defended on Libertarian Grounds?," Reason.com, April 8, 2015.
Jerry Taylor	"Libertarian Principles & Climate Change," Niskanen Center, April 6, 2015.

Chapter 4

How Do Libertarians View Other American Issues?

Chapter Preface

The heart of American libertarianism lies in its support of nearly any political position that limits the power of the federal government in favor of allowing the American people to live their lives freely, without fear of the state encroaching into their personal decisions. Some libertarian stances, such as supporting the full legalization of same-sex marriage across the United States, have been praised by Democrats, gay activist groups, and other liberals. Other libertarian positions are viewed by the American political mainstream as too marginal and idiosyncratic to receive much significant attention. One of these positions is the libertarian call for the legalization of marijuana.

Libertarians make a two-pronged case for a complete reform of US marijuana laws. First, they claim, the criminalization of marijuana prevents those Americans suffering from debilitating illnesses such as cancer, AIDS, and glaucoma from using the drug to alleviate chronic pain. According to libertarians, the nationwide decriminalization of marijuana would allow these people to acquire medicinal amounts of the substance so they could increase their qualities of life and possibly even avoid death.

The second aspect of the libertarian case for marijuana decriminalization involves criminal justice and the American prison system. The Libertarian Party asserts that more than 658,000 Americans are arrested each year for possessing marijuana. Libertarians claim these people are otherwise law-abiding citizens who are now in prison, separated from their loved ones, while American taxpayers have paid more than $1 trillion for the incarceration of such persons since 1971. Libertarians argue that recreational marijuana use is a personal decision that harms no one and, therefore, should not be a labeled a criminal act. America's war on drugs has proven to be an utter failure, libertarians claim, as marijuana use has continued even as arrests and incarcerations have persisted.

The Libertarian Party proposes a singular solution to all of these problems: the decriminalization of marijuana. This would lead, in the party's view, to a domino effect of positive changes for America. First, the federal government's Drug Enforcement Administration would be abolished. Then, every nonviolent drug offender in the United States, totaling more than 500,000 in 2014, would be released from prison, whereupon they could reunite with their families. The sudden release of such a high volume of prisoners would, in turn, heavily reduce taxes on the American populace, as it would no longer need to pay for their incarceration. Finally, according to the party's plan, drug crime would decrease substantially, and police across the country could devote more time and effort to combating violent crime such as murder and robbery. To libertarians, an end to the US drug war would signify the beginning of a new era of justice for the American people.

The following chapter presents opposing viewpoints on various libertarian political positions. Topics discussed include American isolationism, police militarization, mandatory child vaccinations, and the controversy surrounding the legalization of marijuana in the United States.

VIEWPOINT 1

> *"Should the United States abandon its place of leadership in international relations, it would pave the way to destruction of the international order it has striven to build."*

Libertarian Isolationism Would Endanger America

John Engle

In the following viewpoint, John Engle contends that the type of isolationism espoused by libertarians would place the United States, and the world, in more danger. He rejects the notion that retreating from world affairs would keep America safe; rather, Engle believes, the international community needs the United States for political and economic stability. Engle is president of Almington Capital Inc.

As you read, consider the following questions:

1. Which two American wars does Engle identify as making isolationism sound attractive?

John Engle, "The Case Against Isolationism," *Heartland Institute* (blog), August 3, 2014. http://blog.heartland.org.

2. What does Engle say would happen in the international financial system without the dollar?
3. After what event does Engle say budding democratic movements looked to the United States for inspiration?

There is a strain of thought in the American pro-liberty movement that argues for what is essentially return to a policy of isolationism. That is the attitude typified by former representative Ron Paul and his adherents, who have spent years calling for the withdrawal of the United States from many of its foreign treaty and institutional obligations, including the United Nations. There is a certain attractiveness to this position, especially in light of the recent exhausting and expensive wars in Iraq and Afghanistan. The claim that the war on terror and other interventions in various countries' affairs have created more enemies than they vanquished holds no small amount of truth.

It is true that America has pursued an overbearing and damaging foreign policy in the past two decades. But it is also true that a policy of isolation would be even more damaging.

Pax Americana

The United States occupies a unique position in the history of the world; it is a superpower with the ability to project military power to all corners of the globe and economic capacity dwarfing all other states. Never has a state been so dominant and without rivals for global preeminence. In terms of security, its great power has given the United States the ability to serve as an ersatz world police, allowing it to guarantee the security and stability of the international system, as well as the security of its own citizens, which has resulted in an unprecedented era of peace reigning in the world.

Wars in this era of American preeminence have been intermittent and localized, nothing akin to the vast conflicts of empire that marked the 18th and 19th centuries, or the cata-

Isolationism Increases Terrorism

As a veteran, and as a governor who has supported Texas National Guard deployments to Iraq and Afghanistan, I can understand the emotions behind isolationism. Many people are tired of war, and the urge to pull back is a natural, human reaction. Unfortunately, we live in a world where isolationist policies would only endanger our national security even further.

That's why it's disheartening to hear fellow Republicans, such as Sen. Rand Paul (Ky.), suggest that our nation should ignore what's happening in Iraq. The main problem with this argument is that it means ignoring the profound threat that the group now calling itself the Islamic State [ISIS] poses to the United States and the world. . . .

Ignoring the growth of the Islamic State and events in Syria and Iraq will only ensure that the problem will fester and grow. The United States needs to take seriously the threat this presents to our nation.

Paul is an articulate advocate for his views, which are shared by many on the left and some on the right. But in today's world, with today's threats, we still cannot "take blind shelter across the sea, rushing to respond only after freedom is lost." That was President [Ronald] Reagan's warning. Sen. Paul would be wise to heed it.

Rick Perry, "Isolationist Policies Make the Threat of Terrorism Even Greater," Washington Post, *July 11, 2014.*

clysmic world wars of the first half of the 20th century. This has largely been thanks to the United States' presence as a leader on the world stage. Were it to withdraw from its international activities, the security of the world would be in doubt.

With no dominant power helping to maintain order, the whole system could break down, precipitating wars, as has occurred in previous centuries when the international landscape was marked by the power dynamics of multi-polarity.

In terms of economics, the United States is deeply coupled into the system. The United States' withdrawal as guarantor of the system would be disastrous not only in terms of upsetting the international financial system, but also in terms of its position as provider of the world's reserve currency. Without the dollar, the entire international financial system would be in jeopardy, and could even collapse. Without the United States actively involved on the international stage the world will become a more dangerous and economically volatile place.

The Indispensable Nation

Much of the world looks to the United States for leadership. Its moniker "leader of the free world" is not merely grandstanding on America's part, but actually how many nations view it. In terms of maintenance of the present international order, of which America was the chief architect and guarantor, the United States remains the "indispensable nation."

When the Berlin Wall fell it was to the United States that the budding democratic movements looked for inspiration. Its upholding of values such as freedom of expression and of religion, as well as its adherence to democratic values and free markets have served to shape the fabric of the international order. Since the United States became a major leader in the world, after World War II, it has helped to make the soil of the international landscape become more receptive to the growth of democracy and free market capitalism, not only as a major form of government, but as the predominant one.

Should the United States abandon its place of leadership in international relations, it would pave the way to destruction of the international order it has striven to build. I have previously written about the problems of America's failure to establish an international order that would survive its decline. A policy of isolation like some on the libertarian-right wing of American politics would only hasten that erosion of international norms. The [Barack] Obama administration's rudderless foreign policy leadership should be viewed as a chilling prelude to a world without American leadership. It is a world that should be avoided at all costs.

A Way Forward

The United States is too important to the international system to abandon it. Doing so could result in all manner of catastrophe, not just for other countries, but for the United States as well. The problems of the world cannot simply be sealed off from America's shores, especially if free trade is to still be upheld.

It is in America's interest, and in the interest of the world, that the United States pursue a foreign policy that continues to promote the norms it has sought to inculcate in international relations. The task is not complete, and has seen setbacks in the past few years. But failure is not an option.

Viewpoint 2

> *"Our military should be used for defense, not to police the world."*

America Would Be Safer Not Policing the World

John Stossel

In the following viewpoint, John Stossel argues that the United States would be safer by not increasing its military presence around the world. The country should use its military only to defend itself, Stossel believes, and should learn from its mistakes that foreign intervention can cause many unforeseen problems for the United States. Stossel is the host of Stossel, *a political talk show on the Fox Business Network.*

As you read, consider the following questions:

1. According to Stossel's source, what country should the United States attack if it acquires nuclear weapons?
2. What mistakes does Stossel say the United States made in Iraq after its military campaign there?
3. How much more money does Stossel say Barack Obama spent in Afghanistan than George W. Bush?

John Stossel, "Libertarians Versus Conservatives," Creators.com, June 16, 2014.

Both libertarians and conservatives want to keep America safe. We differ on how best to do that. Most libertarians believe our attempts to create or support democracy around the world have made us new enemies, and done harm as well as good. We want less military spending.

Some conservatives respond to that by calling us isolationists, but we're not. I want to participate in the world; I just don't want to run it. I'm glad Americans trade with other countries—trade both goods and people. It's great we sell foreigners our music, movies, ideas, etc. And through dealing with them, we also learn from what they do best.

The Importance of Image

On my TV show this week [in June 2014], former U.S. ambassador to the UN [United Nations] John Bolton will tell me why my libertarian skepticism about the importance of a "strong military presence" is "completely irrelevant to foreign policy decision making."

Bolton thinks it's dangerous and provocative for America to appear militarily weak. He supported the Iraq War and says that if Iran were close to getting nuclear weapons, the U.S should attack. "I will go to my grave trying to prevent every new country we can find from getting nuclear weapons," because if they do, "it's going to be a very dangerous world."

He criticizes Presidents Barack Obama's and George W. Bush's failed attempts at negotiation with Iran, "negotiation based on the delusion from the get-go that Iran was ever serious about potentially giving up its nuclear weapons program."

That kind of talk makes Bolton sound like a hardheaded realist. Who wants to be naive like Bush or Obama? But hawks like Bolton ignore parts of reality, too.

They are quick and correct to point out the danger of Iran going nuclear. They are not as quick to talk about the fact that Iran has a population three times the size of Iraq's—and the

Americans Support Isolationism

More and more Americans believe that the United States' international power and prestige are waning. For the first time, more than half of Americans oppose their nation's policy of global engagement.

A new survey by Pew [Research Center] published on Wednesday [December 4, 2013] has determined that 52 percent of Americans think that the U.S. "should mind its own business internationally and let other countries get along the best they can on their own," while only 38 percent disagree with that statement.

These figures represent the highest amount of support for isolationist policy in the U.S. since the Pew Research Center began conducting this survey 50 years ago. For comparison, in 1976, the year after the Vietnam War ended, only 42 percent of Americans believed that their nation should reduce its involvement in international affairs. . . .

However, despite the opposition to U.S. involvement in world affairs, most Americans support a global economy. 77 percent see economic ties and deals with other countries as beneficial to the U.S.

Haaretz and Associated Press,
"World's Policeman Looking to Retire: American Support for Isolationism Hits 50-Year High, PEW Survey Finds,"
Haaretz, December 5, 2013.

Iraq War wasn't as smooth or short as then vice president Dick Cheney and others assured us it would be.

If it's realistic to acknowledge that America has dangerous enemies, it's also realistic to acknowledge that going to war is not always worth the loss of money and lives, and that it makes *new* enemies. War, like most government plans, tends not to work out as well as planners hoped.

I asked Bolton if he thought the Vietnam War was a good intervention. "Obviously, the way it played out, it was not," he said, but, "it's always easy after the fact to second-guess."

Bolton also acknowledges that the Iraq War did not go well, but then adds, "Where mistakes were made was *after* the military campaign." The U.S. was unprepared for the civil war that broke out. The U.S. also failed to turn utilities and other state-run companies in Iraq over to the private sector, maintaining poorly run monopolies on energy production and other essential services, often squandering billions of dollars.

The Dangers of Policing

It might be seen as a harsh lesson in the importance of planning for the aftermath of toppling a bad regime. But we libertarians wonder: Why assume government will do better next time?

Occasionally government acknowledges mistakes in domestic policy—but that doesn't mean it then becomes more efficient. It usually just spends *more* to try, and fail, to fix the problem. It's the nature of government. Politicians don't face the competitive incentives that force other people to make hard decisions.

Candidate Obama garnered support by criticizing Bush for costing money and lives through a protracted stay in Iraq. But that didn't stop Obama from putting more money and troops into Afghanistan.

In his first term alone, Obama spent about three times as much in Afghanistan as Bush did in two terms. Did we win hearts and minds? I don't think so. The Taliban may still retake the country.

Our military should be used for defense, not to police the world.

Viewpoint 3

> *"The distribution of arms among the police . . . fails to supply a single warrant for the charge of 'militarization.'"*

Libertarians Are Wrong on Police Militarization

Jack Kerwick

In the following viewpoint, Jack Kerwick argues that it is incorrect to call America's police militarized. The simple possession of heavy weapons, he believes, does not constitute militarization, as many American citizens have access to the same firearms as police. Ultimately, Kerwick writes, police are only doing their jobs when they use their military equipment to stop criminals. Kerwick is a writer for FrontPage Magazine.

As you read, consider the following questions:

1. What is Kerwick's response to libertarian objections that the police are using their military power for the coercion of citizens?
2. What does Kerwick say is an exception to charges of police coercion with military equipment?

Jack Kerwick, "The 'Militarization' of the Police?," FrontPageMag.com, September 3, 2014.

3. What other police crimes does Kerwick say should not be confused with militarization?

Making the rounds through libertarian (and other) circles in the wake of the police shooting death of Michael Brown is the notion that the "militarization" of local police forces is a huge problem besetting the country.

Though I self-identify as a conservative, I have a considerable affection for libertarianism. In fact, it is precisely because of this fondness that I am compelled to put out to pasture all of this "militarization" talk.

Mere Possession

(1) The mere possession of weaponry of a kind on the part of police is no more objectionable—no more a justification for the charge of "militarization"—than is the mere existence of guns or SUVs objectionable.

For starters, it is unclear as to what libertarians even mean in claiming that the police are "militarized." From what I can gather—sorry, but no self-avowed libertarian writer who I have yet encountered is clear on this—it is the fact that today's police forces are equipped with weaponry of a technologically sophisticated sort, the sort with which our soldiers are armed when confronting enemies overseas, that warrants the charge of "militarization."

How the mere possession of things is a cause of alarm for, of all people, the libertarian, is beyond me. In personifying inanimate objects he comes perilously close to sounding like just those enemies of liberty against whom he's tirelessly railing, those who would personify guns, wealth, and, say, SUVs.

Moreover, libertarians are the first to champion the (law-abiding, adult) citizen's constitutional, even "inalienable," right to bear virtually whatever arms he prefers. How, we must ask, does it turn out to be permissible—not "militarized"—for the janitor next door to possess a machine gun, but somehow impermissible—"militarized"—for the police to do the same?

Distribution of Arms

(2) The distribution of arms among the police, on the one hand, and the citizenry, on the other, utterly fails to establish that the police, or anyone, haven't a right to arm themselves like Rambo—i.e., it fails to supply a single warrant for the charge of "militarization."

If the libertarian insists that it isn't the possession by police of weaponry as such to which he objects, but the fact that, as things currently stand, the police have access to these weapons to which other citizens are denied, then it is the distribution of this access, and not the access itself, that has him upset.

But if this is the case, then the proper complaint is not, "The police are 'militarized'!" The proper complaint is that, "We should be allowed to be 'militarized' too," or something like this.

In other words, the charge of "militarization" makes no sense here.

Insufficient Coercion

(3) The concept of "militarization" encompasses the concepts of collective purpose and coercion.

Government, by definition, has a monopoly on force. Yet, theoretically, the libertarian, unlike the anarchist, has no objections to this: The libertarian recognizes the authority of government to both enact and enforce laws. Since police officers are government agents, the libertarian affirms their authority to deploy the power at their disposal to coerce citizens into abiding by the laws that police are committed to safeguarding.

So, the sheer fact that police are endowed with the power to coerce prospective and actual violators of the law can't be something with which the libertarian has a problem, for he has no problem with government per se.

In other words, that police are using force to maintain law and order—precisely what police have always done and what they've always been meant to do—can't be the spring of the libertarian's howls of "militarization."

Only if government agents—whether police or otherwise—are coercing citizens in the service of fulfilling some grand collective purpose will the charge of "militarization" apply. Coercion, in and of itself, is insufficient to constitute "militarization."

But this, in turn, means that the actual weaponry with which the police (or any other agent of the government) are endowed is irrelevant to determining whether the police, or any other agent of government, are "militarized." If police were armed only with clubs, but used these clubs in order to insure that citizens were exercising three days a week for the purpose of producing "The Physically Fit Society," say, then this would indeed show that the police had a "militarized" set of mind. Conversely, if the police are armed to the teeth with the stuff of soldiers but used their arms only to insure that the rule of law was preserved, to protect the life, limb, and property of citizens from those—like the rioters in Ferguson [city in Missouri, where protests broke out after the shooting of Michael Brown, a young, unarmed black man, by a white police officer]—who are intent upon undermining civilization, this would fail to establish that they are "militarized."

Conflating Issues

(4) Police brutality, dereliction of duty, abuse of power and the like are issues that should count for much for all decent people, especially the libertarian. But none of these things are necessarily a function of "militarization," much less equivalent to it.

That there are police officers that abuse their authority and power is not only an empirically verified fact; it is a no-brainer to the lover of liberty who knows, along with Lord Acton, that while "absolute power tends to corrupt absolutely," even a limited degree of "power tends to corrupt."

But when police do violate their oath to serve and protect, then we can and should call out their violations for what they are. Conflating or obscuring issues with bumper-sticker-friendly misnomers like "militarization" is counterproductive.

VIEWPOINT 4

"The only fair libertarian position is that you . . . should not be allowed to introduce yourself or your children into the public arena unless you vaccinate."

Libertarians Must Support Mandatory Child Vaccinations

Gary Nolan

In the following viewpoint, Gary Nolan argues for a government mandate making vaccinations against harmful or deadly illnesses mandatory. He refutes objectors' arguments for liberty by claiming that the US government would actually be restricting liberty by allowing its populace to become gravely ill simply because some people chose not to become vaccinated. Nolan is a contributor to The Logical Libertarian *blog.*

As you read, consider the following questions:

1. According to Nolan's research, what is the percentage range of vaccines' effectiveness?
2. What does Nolan say would happen in a community if enough people became vaccinated?

Gary Nolan, "Vaccine or No Vaccine: The Facts and This Libertarian's Opinion," Logical Libertarian.com, February 4, 2015.

3. What does Nolan say is the most important citizen right a government should protect?

The latest litmus test for politicians seems to be the idea of mandatory versus voluntary vaccinations. Even libertarians are somewhat divided on this, but the liberty-minded factions seem to support pro-choice, and the statist-leaning folks are going towards making them mandatory.

Vaccine Basics

First, let's point out that most people agree that vaccinations are one of mankind's greatest medical achievements. Whether you're pro-choice or not, I think we all agree that science has proven them to be overwhelmingly effective.

Rand Paul recently weighed in that he supported a pro-choice position, but he got himself into trouble when he stated, "I have heard of many tragic cases of walking, talking normal children who wound up with profound mental disorders after vaccines."

If I were to give Rand Paul the benefit of the doubt here, I would like to believe he was simply arguing that some people are afraid of vaccines because children have been diagnosed with mental disorders after being vaccinated, as a means to explain why people might not want to vaccinate, even if this is anecdotal evidence, which is definitively not scientific.

I would like to think he was not arguing that there was any causality, since studies have almost universally debunked this myth. But if he was, that is sadly a very unscientific position for someone who is currently practicing medicine to posit. [Editor's note: Paul is a physician who practiced ophthalmology before entering politics.]

While it has been reported that some vaccines may cause temporary issues, I don't think any credible studies have supported the notion that any permanent complications have arisen.

But either way, let's explore what actually happens when you're given a vaccine. A vaccine is essentially a dead, or severely weakened version of a real virus.

To oversimplify things a bit, anything introduced into your body that doesn't have your DNA will be seen by your immune system as a threat, and your immune system will go about trying to destroy it.

This is the reason that your immune system must be suppressed when you receive a donor organ for instance, and why organs harvested from your own DNA are much safer and advantageous.

On a side note, as fantastic as this may sound, I don't think I'm overstating this one iota when I say that this particular field of research will revolutionize the world of medicine forever; we are truly on the cusp of never needing organ donors again.

Think of the vaccine as a new first-person war-simulating video game you just bought. At first, you don't know any of the levels, how to defeat any of the enemies, etc. So you play the game on its easiest mode until you learn the most effective means to slay your enemies. Once you've mastered it, you are ready for the more advanced levels.

This is what vaccines are effectively doing. Because the vaccine is a dead or weak form of the virus, it's like the game on "easy" mode where it's of little to no threat to you. In this state, your body can train itself to kill the virus so it's better prepared to kill the full strength version down the road, if it's introduced into your system.

So why does it not work sometimes? Well, what if the copy of the video game you received was *Halo*, but the real disease is *Call of Duty*? You've prepared for the wrong game. There isn't just one influenza virus, there are various strains. So it's important that the medical field do their research well and introduce a vaccine that prepares you for the influenza strain that is expected to be most prevalent.

Bodily Effects

Now, let's also explore the effects on your body when you get a vaccine. Your immune system is not magic, it uses energy from what you consume—energy you would otherwise use to run, jump, and play.

So it's not uncommon for some short-term effects as your body diverts its resources to the battle you've just entered it into with the vaccine. When you get sick, you get weak also, right? It's because your body is diverting energy to fight the virus you have. Whether it's a vaccine or a live virus, your immune system has a lot of work to do, and you will be affected in that moment.

Since every person is different, people's reactions will vary. Some people might get the vaccine and feel almost nothing, others may get the vaccine and feel like their energy level has been reduced by half. It's for this reason that Rand Paul suggested staggering these immunizations so that your body can tackle one virus at a time to keep the short-term weakening effects to a minimum. Plus, if your immune system is busy fighting one battle, it may not be well suited to fight another, which should make basic sense.

The Politics of Vaccines

Now that we've covered the facts, let's get toward the opinion of whether it should be optional or mandatory.

Vaccines are rather effective, but they're not bulletproof. Depending on the vaccine, you will see here that the CDC [Centers for Disease Control and Prevention] has found the effectiveness to vary anywhere from as low as 59% and as high as 92%. This is the single most important factor I used in forming my opinion.

Some people online have posted memes asking the question, "If vaccines work, and you've had one, why are you concerned if I get one?"

A Call for Mandatory Vaccination

Fox News host Megyn Kelly late Monday [in February 2015] said she supports mandatory vaccinations, an issue that has become increasingly political, after more than 100 cases of measles have been reported in the U.S.

Appearing on *The O'Reilly Factor*, Kelly said she feels there is sufficient scientific evidence to prove vaccines are effective. She added that she vaccinated all of her children, as recommended by their doctor.

"Five years ago, the science wasn't even as certain as it is today," she said. "But it is very certain today."

The issue of whether parents should have the choice to vaccinate their children has caused a political stir among potential GOP 2016 presidential candidates.

New Jersey Gov. Chris Christie and Kentucky Sen. Rand Paul on Monday both said parents should have the freedom to make their own decision. Others, like retired neurosurgeon Ben Carson, stressed that public health and safety should be a priority.

Eric Garland,
"Fox's Megyn Kelly: I Support Mandatory Vaccinations,"
The Hill, *February 3, 2015.*

On the face of it, it seems like a fair question, but it's one borne out of ignorance. As I stated above, at best, they seem about 90% effective. So imagine a scenario that I am interacting with you, and you have the virus in question. If you haven't been vaccinated, there's a 1:9 chance I may get the disease from you. But if you've also been vaccinated, that means my risk now goes from 1:9 to 1:81 (1/9 x 1/9 = 1/81). The more people who get vaccinated, the more the odds go down.

If enough get vaccinated, the odds will eventually exceed the number of people in an area, and the disease will likely be eradicated. Meaning that if the odds of you catching it get to 1:1,000, but there's only 900 people in your community, the odds would then favor eradication of the disease—basic math.

Assuming you're not an anarchist, almost all of us believe government's duties are to protect our rights. Statists think government has many more duties, but I don't know of any non-anarchists championing government causes that don't include protecting rights first. The most important of these rights? The right to life.

So if vaccines are anything less than 100% effective, which they are, government enforcing you to get one isn't for your benefit; it's to protect others from you if you catch the virus.

What so often happens is people want to create a paradox to sound smart, something no one should ever intelligently do. For instance, it's like asking a Christian if God can build a wall so high even he can't climb it—a purely nonsensical question.

Arguing that vaccines should be a choice creates a similar liberty paradox. Because while you're giving liberty to one person, you're effectively taking it away from everyone else they'll come in contact with, which mathematically, is a net loss for liberty.

It would be no different from arguing that slavery should be legal because it gives liberty to the slave owner, or as Greg Gutfeld pointed out (I don't want to take credit for his argument), it would be like legalizing drinking and driving because you're restoring liberty to the future AA [Alcoholics Anonymous] member.

The only way you are truly for liberty is if you champion the view that gives the greatest amount of liberty. Giving one person liberty while denying the rights of ten others, is not a libertarian position, it's a selfish one, in my opinion.

Now, you can rightfully argue I've created my own liberty paradox by denying the right of the anti-vaccine person, but I have an answer for that. If they choose to self-quarantine in some way, then by all means, let them not vaccinate. I'm perfectly OK with that—problem solved, paradox gone.

Otherwise, I think the only fair libertarian position is that you cannot own a slave, you cannot drink and drive, you cannot drive a car without insurance to cover me if you hit me, and as much as I hate government mandates, I feel you should not be allowed to introduce yourself or your children into the public arena unless you vaccinate.

Viewpoint 5

"The large majority of Americans can use marijuana and guns responsibly."

Libertarian Support for Legalizing Marijuana Is Good for America

Michael Barone

In the following viewpoint, Michael Barone argues that recent libertarian swings toward issues such as marijuana legalization, same-sex marriage, and gun rights are good for America, as they promote the exercise of individual freedom. To those who still worry about these matters, Barone writes, Americans have shown restraint in participating in these controversial activities, proving that the activities' potential dangers can always be tempered with responsibility. Barone is a contributor to Fox News.

As you read, consider the following questions:

1. What two states does Barone say approved of same-sex marriage in November of 2012?
2. What does Barone say is the relationship of young Americans to their elders in regard to abortion rights?

3. What problems does Barone still see at the bottom of America's social scale?

Are Americans becoming more libertarian on cultural issues? I see evidence that they are, in poll findings and election results on three unrelated issues—marijuana legalization, same-sex marriage and gun rights.

Movements Toward Legalization

Start with pot. Last November [2012] voters in the states of Colorado and Washington voted to legalize marijuana, by a 55 to 45 percent margin in Colorado (more than Barack Obama's margin in the state) and by 56 to 44 percent in Washington.

In contrast, California voters rejected legalization 53 to 47 percent in 2010. These results and poll data suggest a general movement toward legal marijuana.

State legislatures in Denver and Olympia have been grappling with regulatory legislation amid uncertainty over whether federal law—and federal law enforcers—override their state laws.

But marijuana has already become effectively legal in many of the states that have reduced penalties for possession of small amounts or have legalized medical marijuana. You can easily find addresses and phone numbers of dispensaries on the web.

Same-sex marriage, rejected in statewide votes between 1998 and 2008 and most recently in North Carolina in May 2012, was approved by voters in Maine and Maryland in November 2012, and voters then rejected a ban on it in Minnesota.

Since then, legislators in Delaware, Minnesota and Rhode Island have voted to legalize same-sex marriage. A dozen states and the District of Columbia now have similar laws that would have been unthinkable two decades ago.

I have yet to see signs of political backlash. Polls show that support for same-sex marriage is well-nigh universal among young Americans, but it has also been rising among their elders.

To some it may seem odd to yoke together marijuana and gay rights, generally thought of as causes of the left, with gun rights, supported more by the political right. Yet in all three cases, Americans have been moving toward greater liberty for the individual.

One landmark was the first law, passed in Florida in 1987, allowing ordinary citizens to carry concealed weapons. Many, including me, thought that the result would be frequent shootouts in the streets.

That hasn't happened. It turns out that almost all ordinary citizens handle guns with appropriate restraint, as they do with the other potential deadly weapon people encounter every day, the automobile.

Concealed-carry laws have spread to 40 states, with few ill effects. Politicians who opposed them initially, like former Michigan Gov. Jennifer Granholm, have not sought their repeal.

In contrast, voters have reacted negatively to gun control proposals, even after horrific events like the Newtown massacre [referring to the Connecticut school shooting that killed twenty-six people]. That was apparent in the Senate's rejection of the [Pat] Toomey–[Joe] Manchin gun registration bill.

What about the cultural issue that most pundits mention first, abortion? Attitudes have remained roughly the same: Most Americans think abortion should be, in Bill Clinton's phrase, safe, legal and rare.

Young Americans, contrary to their libertarian leaning on same-sex marriage, are slightly less pro-abortion rights than their elders. They've seen sonograms, and all of them by definition owe their existence to a decision not to abort.

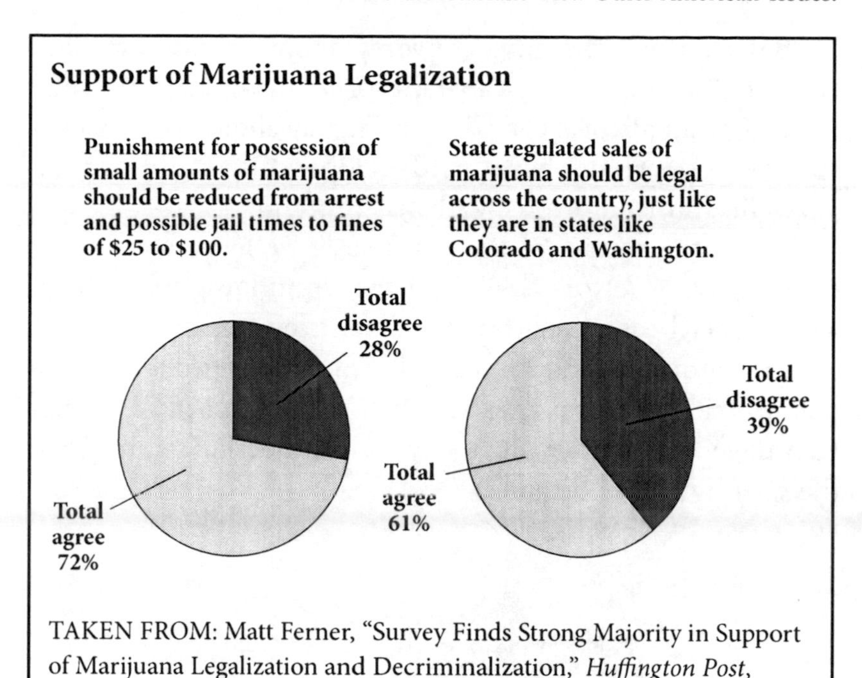

TAKEN FROM: Matt Ferner, "Survey Finds Strong Majority in Support of Marijuana Legalization and Decriminalization," *Huffington Post*, March 18, 2015.

And from the point of view of the unborn child, abortion is the opposite of liberating.

The Libertarian Trend

Back in the conformist America of the 1950s—a nation of greater income equality and stronger labor unions, as liberals like to point out—marijuana, homosexual acts and abortion weren't political issues. They were crimes. And opposition to gun control measures in the 1950s and 1960s was much less widespread and vigorous than it is today.

Is this libertarian trend a good thing for the nation? Your answer will depend on your values.

I'm inclined to look favorably on it. I think the large majority of Americans can use marijuana and guns responsibly. Same-sex marriage can be seen as liberating, but it also includes an element of restraint. Abortions in fact have become more rare over a generation.

But I do see something to worry about. In his best seller *Coming Apart*, my American Enterprise Institute [for Public Policy Research] colleague Charles Murray shows that college-educated Americans have handled liberating trends of the 1970s like no-fault divorce with self-restraint.

But at the bottom of the social scale we have seen an unraveling, with out-of-wedlock births, continuing joblessness, lack of social connectedness and civic involvement.

In conformist America the old prohibitions provided these people with guardrails, as the *Wall Street Journal*'s Daniel Henninger has written. In today's more libertarian America, the guardrails may be gone.

VIEWPOINT 6

> *"It should come as no surprise that marijuana use among American teenagers is rising at an alarming rate—just as efforts to decriminalize it are accelerating."*

Marijuana Should Not Be Legalized

J. Lee Grady

In the following viewpoint, J. Lee Grady argues that marijuana can cause a range of health problems for those who use it, and, therefore, the drug should not be legalized. Aside from this, he contends, frequent marijuana use has been shown to lead to the general depreciation of the lives of users, from depression to poverty. Grady is director of the Mortdecai Project.

As you read, consider the following questions:

1. According to Grady, what are the symptoms of people who have tried to stop using marijuana?
2. What does the National Institute on Drug Abuse report can happen to the mental health of regular marijuana users?

J. Lee Grady, "5 Reasons Why Legalizing Marijuana Stinks," CharismaNews.com, January 16, 2014.

3. What symptoms does Grady say occur after marijuana smokers experience highs?

Have you smelled anything strange in the wind lately? In case you haven't noticed, our nation is literally going to pot. We might as well get used to the odor. Marijuana laws are changing. The drug has been decriminalized in many states, while others allow marijuana use for medicinal purposes only.

At the beginning of January [2014], Colorado citizens were allowed to buy pot for recreational use from authorized dealers. Now tourists are lining up to visit the state for "marijuana vacations." They will no doubt bring new meaning to Colorado's official song, "Rocky Mountain High."

Major Concerns

People from every side of the political spectrum have called for decriminalization of pot—from Pat Robertson and Sarah Palin on the right to Bill Maher and Rachel Maddow on the left. I understand their concern: Huge numbers of people are in prison today for drug possession—and the cost of caring for our inmate population is overwhelming. But why do we have to swing the pendulum to the other extreme and treat marijuana like it's a mild, over-the-counter medication?

Honest health care providers will tell you that marijuana is really bad for you. Legalizing it will only cause its negative effects to increase. If you know anyone who's smoking weed or hoping to start smoking it once it is decriminalized, please pass along these facts.

1. Marijuana is highly addictive. There's a reason marijuana is the most widely used illegal drug in the world. People can't stop using it once they start. Proponents of legalizing pot have tried to dismiss this argument. But clinical studies have proven that people who used marijuana several times a week found it almost impossible to quit. People who tried to stop smoking it reported feeling moody, tense, anxious and unable to sleep.

Opponents of Legal Marijuana Cite Dangers to Individuals and Society

Among the 44% who think marijuana should be illegal, main reason why you feel this way.

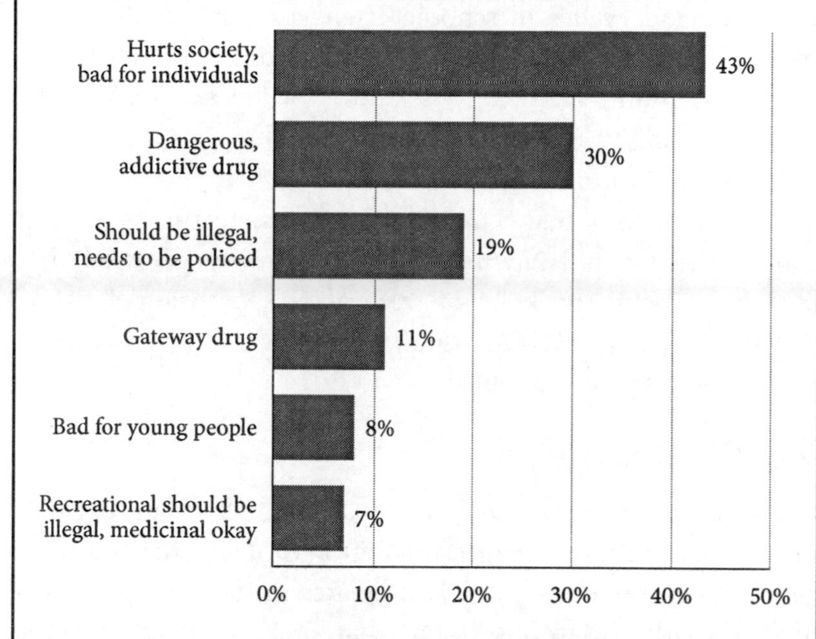

Survey conducted March 25–29, 2015.
Open-ended question. Total exceeds 100% because of multiple responses.

TAKEN FROM: Pew Research Center, "In Debate Over Legalizing Marijuana, Disagreement Over Drug's Dangers," April 14, 2015.

2. *Marijuana can ruin your future.* There is a reason marijuana addicts are sometimes called potheads. The drug sucks the life out of people. Those who use it regularly are more likely to drop out of school, have accidents, quit jobs, lose interest in life and feel generally demotivated. Some studies also have linked pot to suicidal thoughts. The National Institute on Drug Abuse notes that regular marijuana use can result in a 40 percent increased risk of psychosis, and the drug also can lead to schizophrenia, depression and anxiety disorders.

3. Marijuana can ruin your kids' lives. It should come as no surprise that marijuana use among American teenagers is rising at an alarming rate—just as efforts to decriminalize it are accelerating. There has been an 80 percent increase in marijuana use among teens since 2008. Do you want your children to make good grades in school? Then you should know that one study proved that teens who smoked pot regularly lost as much as 8 points in their IQs—and they did not recover the intellectual ability when they became adults.

Parents should also filter through the hype about how marijuana is "not that dangerous." An article published last year in the journal *Neuropsychopharmacology* showed that adolescents who smoked pot were at risk of brain damage. (MEMO TO YOUTH PASTORS: Please devote some time to educating your teens about drugs in 2014.)

Health and Safety

4. Marijuana causes serious health problems. The main ingredient in marijuana, tetrahydrocannabinol, or THC, has a powerful effect on the brain. Initially it creates in the user a sense of euphoria—the infamous "high" that includes bright colors, hallucinations and even laughter. But after the high comes a wave of anxiety, fear and depression. And memory can be affected permanently.

But that's not all. Smoking pot causes a 20 to 100 percent increase in a smoker's heart rate. Some marijuana users are five times more likely to have a heart attack after they use it. Pot is not good for the lungs either. One study found that smoking one joint gives as much exposure to cancer-causing chemicals as smoking five cigarettes. (And you can't help but wonder how secondhand marijuana smoke will affect those of us who are breathing the nearby fumes.)

5. Marijuana can ruin your sex life. Proponents of legalizing marijuana push the idea that pot is an aphrodisiac. But science tells another story. Men who smoke pot regularly can experience impotence as well as infertility. And some studies have found a link between marijuana use and an aggressive form of testicular cancer in young men. Not to mention that pot causes really bad breath. Marijuana is definitely not sexy!

I should also mention that seven percent of drivers involved in accidents tested positive for THC in a recent survey. That's because smoking weed impairs motor skills and increases the risk of car crashes. So if marijuana use becomes widespread after its legalization, we need to be concerned about an increased number of drugged drivers on our roads. Welcome to America—land of the free, home of the stoned.

Please spread the word. Marijuana is called a "weed" for a reason. It's bad for kids. It's bad for adults. When I look at the crazy laws being passed in the United States today, I can't help but wonder what our leaders are smoking.

Periodical and Internet Sources Bibliography

The following articles have been selected to supplement the diverse views presented in this chapter.

John Gizzi	"Libertarians: 'War on Drugs,' 'Law and Order' Caused Firestorm," Newsmax, August 18, 2014.
Michael Harrington	"My Disagreement with Libertarians About Marijuana," RedState.com, January 15, 2014.
Sharon Harris	"Libertarians Are Actually Less 'Isolationist' than Other Political Views," Advocates for Self-Government, January 8, 2015.
Nicholas Kristof	"The Dangers of Vaccine Denial," *New York Times*, February 7, 2015.
Alex MacGillis	"Libertarians Who Oppose a Militarized Police Should Support Gun Control—but They Don't, of Course," *New Republic*, August 21, 2014.
Cory Massimino	"Libertarianism For and Against War," Antiwar .com, May 6, 2015.
Jake Novak	"A Libertarian Argument FOR Vaccine Laws," CNBC, February 10, 2015.
Rand Paul	"Rand Paul: We Must Demilitarize the Police," *Time*, August 14, 2014.
Laurence M. Vance	"Why Libertarians Are Right About Drugs," LewRockwell.com, June 26, 2014.
John P. Walters	"Why Libertarians Are Wrong About Drugs," *Politico*, June 16, 2014.
Matt Welch et al.	"In Search of Libertarian Realism," *Reason*, January 2015.

For Further Discussion

Chapter 1

1. The Daily Take Team excoriates libertarians for wanting to dismantle all government programs that help those in need, such as Medicare and Medicaid. While the author claims this is because libertarians do not care about struggling Americans, libertarians would respond that they are attempting only to remove government from Americans' lives, where it does not belong. Do you believe libertarians want to make the poor suffer, or would the abolishment of welfare programs that help the poor be only an unintended side effect of libertarians' limited-government agenda? Explain your reasoning.
2. Damon Linker states that America is becoming more libertarian—not in politics and government but in morality and culture. Is his argument sound? Does a growing cultural movement signify real change, or must change ultimately fuse to government and legislation for a country to effect actual reforms? Explain.

Chapter 2

1. Laurence M. Vance writes that libertarians are correct in saying the American government should not be providing welfare of any kind to the poor, for this involves the forcible taking of funds from some to give to others. Vance claims this does not imply a libertarian disregard for the poor, only that libertarians want to stop the broadening role of government in Americans' lives. What do you think of Vance's reasoning? Is the principle of shrinking the government worth the suffering that could be incurred by cutting funding to the poor? Why, or why not?

2. Benjamin Studebaker believes the libertarian idea of taxes being theft is wrong, as governments need coercive taxes to rectify inherent societal inequality. Do you think this is a good idea? Should people be forced to forfeit some of their income for the greater good of their society? Or should the principles of individualism, in which people keep all they earn through their own efforts, outweigh those of communalism? Explain your reasoning.
3. Jeremy Griffith supports the libertarian plan to replace America's welfare programs with a basic income guarantee, which would provide $10,000 a year to all American adults over age twenty-two while saving the country more than $1 trillion. Do you think distributing free, universal money is a good idea? Do those who choose not to work deserve this money as much as struggling laborers, or is evenness and fairness always best? Explain.

Chapter 3

1. Kristen Hatten asserts the libertarian nonaggression principle to argue why she thinks libertarians should be pro-life, as abortion is the killing of an innocent human being. She claims that this principle trumps all others at all times, including the right of the mother to exert her own personal freedom by having an abortion. Which do you believe takes precedence: the unborn child's right to life or the mother's right to control her body? Explain.
2. Anthony James Kidwell believes Americans' religious liberty should protect them from not accepting or associating with same-sex marriage to any degree, while some libertarians describe this as discrimination. Should sincere religious convictions legitimize discrimination, or is social equality more important than religion? Explain your reasoning.
3. Chris Berg supports open borders for all nations as a means of ensuring economic liberty for those who seek

better opportunities in other nations. Do you think this is a practical idea? Should countries grant everyone unrestricted access to their territories in the interest of personal liberty? What negative consequences might this have on safety, security, and the world economy?

Chapter 4

1. John Engle believes that isolationism would create grave international danger for America, as the country's sudden retreat from global affairs would produce political instability and wars around the world. Do you believe a constant American presence in the rest of the world is essential to international security, or do you think American interference in the matters of other nations creates more problems than it solves? Explain.
2. Jack Kerwick argues that police militarization is an entirely separate issue from police brutality and abuse of power. He claims the use of excessive force by American police is always wrong but should not be mislabeled as militarization. Do you think his reasoning is valid? Do the militaristic weapons of America's police make police crimes worse, or are the issues truly unrelated? Explain.
3. J. Lee Grady believes the legalization of marijuana in America would be extremely detrimental to public health, as the drug can produce a range of negative effects on the human body. Should the common good of preserving Americans' health be a legitimate concern of the US government, or does this prospect represent what libertarians call the paternalism of big government? Explain your reasoning.

Organizations to Contact

The editors have compiled the following list of organizations concerned with the issues debated in this book. The descriptions are derived from materials provided by the organizations. All have publications or information available for interested readers. The list was compiled on the date of publication of the present volume; the information provided here may change. Be aware that many organizations take several weeks or longer to respond to inquiries, so allow as much time as possible.

Americans for Limited Government
10332 Main Street, Box 326, Fairfax, VA 22030
(703) 383-0880 • fax: (703) 383-5288
e-mail: info@getliberty.org
website: www.getliberty.org

Americans for Limited Government is a libertarian research organization that advocates for the shrinking of the United States federal government. The group believes that when a government contracts and saves money, the freedoms of its citizens increase. Through original research and blog posts, Americans for Limited Government attempts to advance this cause in the American public. Articles from the organization's blog, *NetRightDaily*, can be accessed online at NetRightDaily .com. Titles from this site include "Medicaid's Death Tax on the Poor" and "Slow Economy or Snow Economy?"

Campaign for Liberty
5211 Port Royal Road, Suite 310, Springfield, VA 22151
(703) 865-7162 • fax: (703) 865-7549
website: www.campaignforliberty.org

The Campaign for Liberty was founded by twelve-term US congressman from Texas Ron Paul, a staunch libertarian who has advocated for limited government, free markets, and individual liberties. The organization seeks to educate Washington politicians and the American public about the dangers of a powerful central government, unsound currency, and the erosion of Americans' civil liberties. Its website provides links to libertarian-minded books and news articles, including *The Tea Party Goes to Washington*, by Republican US senator Rand Paul, and *Now or Never: Saving America from Economic Collapse*, by former Republican US senator Jim DeMint.

Cato Institute
1000 Massachusetts Avenue NW
Washington, DC 20001-5403
(202) 842-0200 • fax: (202) 842-3490
website: www.cato.org

The Cato Institute is a libertarian think tank that advocates for limited government involvement in social and economic matters and favors a free market economy. Cato promotes unhindered civil liberties for all Americans, so long as no individual's actions infringe upon the rights of another individual. The organization supports the traditional libertarian belief that anything that does not harm someone else should be permitted in society. Cato's main publication is the *Cato Journal*, which recommends American domestic policy from a libertarian perspective. Copies of Cato studies, reports, and commentaries concerning the status of libertarianism in the United States can be accessed on the organization's website.

Center for Individual Freedom (CFIF)
815 King Street, Suite 303, Alexandria, VA 22314
(703) 535-5836 • fax: (703) 535-5838
e-mail: info@cfif.org
website: www.cfif.org

The Center for Individual Freedom (CFIF) is a nonpartisan research organization devoted to disseminating awareness of the individual liberties granted to Americans through the US Constitution and Bill of Rights. The group does this by engaging with legal authorities who have the power of upholding the civil rights of American citizens; advocating for legislative change in state and federal government; and educating the public on the Constitution through publications, seminars, and news briefings. The CFIF's main publication is its blog, *Freedom Line*, through which the organization's staff writes about various political events throughout the United States, all with the aim of promoting freedom for all American citizens. Articles from this blog can be accessed on the organization's website.

Foundation for Economic Education (FEE)

1718 Peachtree Street NW, Suite #1048, Atlanta, GA 30309
(404) 554-9980 • fax: (404) 393-3142
e-mail: support@fee.org
website: www.fee.org

Founded in 1946, the Foundation for Economic Education (FEE) is an educational organization dedicated to advocating for free economic markets and the maximizing of individual liberties in society. The nonpartisan, but libertarian-leaning group, accomplishes its agenda with seminars, lectures, and researched content both online and in printed form. FEE's main print publication is the *Freeman*, a magazine containing informational articles on free markets, noninterventionism, and the value of individuals. Articles from the *Freeman* are available online and include titles such as "Health Insurance Is Illegal" and "The Berlin Wall: Those Who Refused to Be Caged."

FreedomWorks

400 North Capitol Street NW, Suite 765
Washington, DC 20001
(202) 783-3870
website: www.freedomworks.org

FreedomWorks is a libertarian think tank and advocacy group that espouses the importance of individual freedoms and free economic markets in contemporary America. This grassroots organization is composed of more than six million members who attempt to engage with state and federal politicians directly, making known their desires for limited government, lower taxes, and an end to government involvement in private industry. FreedomWorks' main news outlet is its own FreedomConnector, which provides links to news articles and blog posts submitted by FreedomWorks supporters.

Independent Institute
100 Swan Way, Oakland, CA 94621-1428
(510) 632-1366 • fax: (510) 568-6040
website: www.independent.org

The Independent Institute is a nonpartisan research organization that seeks to educate the American public about the tenets of classical libertarianism. These include peace, economic prosperity, and maximum freedom for the individual. The Independent Institute prolifically researches and produces scholarly criticism on current US policy. The organization's quarterly journal is the *Independent Review*, which features peer-reviewed articles on libertarian themes reagrding economics, politics, and policy decisions. The institute's quarterly newsletter is the *Independent*, which contains news and opinion articles on various political issues. Links to articles in these publications, as well as to policy reports, working papers, and other information sheets, can be accessed on the Independent Institute's website.

Libertarian Party
1444 Duke Street, Alexandria, VA 22314-3403
(202) 333-0008 • fax: (202) 333-0072
website: www.lp.org

Since its founding in 1971, the Libertarian Party has worked to return America to its original state under the Founding Fathers. This involves the promotion of a small central government that does not become involved in the personal lives of its citizens. The party also supports maximum civil liberties for all Americans, including the people's rights to procure abortions, marry anyone they choose, engage in free markets, and use marijuana. The party holds a national convention every year and has consistently nominated its own candidates for president and vice president since 1972. The Libertarian Party's main publication is *LP News*, a bimonthly newspaper covering the activities of party members around the country. Past issues of *LP News* are available on the Libertarian Party's website.

Mises Institute

518 West Magnolia Avenue, Auburn, AL 36832-4501
(334) 321-2100 • fax: (334) 321-2119
website: www.mises.org

The Mises Institute is a libertarian organization dedicated to educating the American public in Austrian economics, an academic school that promotes free markets with no government involvement. This is part of the larger libertarian framework supported by the institute as the best political course for the United States. Other classical libertarian positions advanced by the organization include maximized individual freedoms, the principle of nonaggression, and the supremacy of private property. The Mises Institute publishes numerous volumes of libertarian economic news and criticism. Chief among these are the *Mises Daily*, which uses Austrian economics to examine current and past events, and the *Austrian*, a bimonthly magazine that applies Austrian theory to contemporary American policy. Articles from these sources and more can be accessed on the Mises website.

Reason Foundation

5737 Mesmer Avenue, Los Angeles, CA 90230
(310) 391-2245
website: www.reason.org

The Reason Foundation is a research group that promotes the introduction of libertarian policies to American life. It supports the removal of the federal government from numerous aspects of American society, including health care, education, and air transportation. The organization suggests instead the privatization of these and other institutions. The Reason

Foundation's primary publication is *Reason* magazine, published monthly as a conduit for the group's libertarian agenda. Reason.com features daily articles and columns on current developments in politics and culture and provides the full text of past issues of the print edition of *Reason* magazine.

Bibliography of Books

Radley Balko	*The Militarization of America's Police Forces*. New York: PublicAffairs, 2013.
Wes Benedict	*Introduction to the Libertarian Party: For Democrats, Republicans, Libertarians, Independents, and Everyone Else*. Seattle, WA: CreateSpace, 2013.
David Boaz, ed.	*The Libertarian Reader: Classic & Contemporary Writings from Lao-Tzu to Milton Friedman*. New York: Simon & Schuster, 2015.
Jason Brennan	*Libertarianism: What Everyone Needs to Know*. New York: Oxford University Press, 2012.
Charles C.W. Cooke	*The Conservatarian Manifesto: Libertarians, Conservatives, and the Fight for the Right's Future*. New York: Crown Forum, 2015.
Jay Cost	*A Republic No More: Big Government and the Rise of American Political Corruption*. New York: Encounter Books, 2015.
Brian Doherty	*Radicals for Capitalism: A Freewheeling History of the Modern American Libertarian Movement*. New York: PublicAffairs, 2008.
Randy England	*Free Is Beautiful: Why Catholics Should Be Libertarian*. Seattle, WA: CreateSpace, 2012.

Nick Gillespie and Matt Welch	*The Declaration of Independents: How Libertarian Politics Can Fix What's Wrong with America*. New York: PublicAffairs, 2011.
Louise Kuo Habakus and Mary Holland, eds.	*Vaccine Epidemic: How Corporate Greed, Biased Science, and Coercive Government Threaten Our Human Rights, Our Health, and Our Children*. New York: Skyhorse Publishing, 2011.
Edward Hudgins, ed.	*The Republican Party's Civil War: Will Freedom Win?* New York: Atlas Society, 2014.
Georgia Kelly, ed.	*Uncivil Liberties: Deconstructing Libertarianism*. Sonoma, CA: Praxis Peace Institute, 2013.
Matt Kibbe	*Don't Hurt People and Don't Take Their Stuff: A Libertarian Manifesto*. New York: William Morrow, 2014.
Mike Lofgren	*The Party Is Over: How Republicans Went Crazy, Democrats Became Useless, and the Middle Class Got Shafted*. New York: Viking Adult, 2012.
Paula Mallea	*The War on Drugs: A Failed Experiment*. Toronto, ON: Dundurn, 2014.
Jeffrey A. Miron	*Libertarianism, from A to Z*. New York: Basic Books, 2010.

Charles Murray	*By the People: Rebuilding Liberty Without Permission*. New York: Crown Forum, 2015.
Anthony Pagden	*The Enlightenment: And Why It Still Matters*. New York: Random House, 2013.
Rand Paul	*Taking a Stand: Moving Beyond Partisan Politics to Unite America*. New York: Center Street, 2015.
Ron Paul	*Liberty Defined: 50 Essential Issues That Affect Our Freedom*. New York: Grand Central Publishing, 2012.
Katha Pollitt	*Pro: Reclaiming Abortion Rights*. New York: Picador, 2014.
Daniel Schulman	*Sons of Wichita: How the Koch Brothers Became America's Most Powerful and Private Dynasty*. New York: Grand Central Publishing, 2014.
David Sehat	*The Jefferson Rule: How the Founding Fathers Became Infallible and Our Politics Inflexible*. New York: Simon & Schuster, 2015.
Allan Sheahen	*Basic Income Guarantee: Your Right to Economic Security*. New York: Palgrave Macmillan, 2012.
Larry Siedentop	*Inventing the Individual: The Origins of Western Liberalism*. Cambridge, MA: Belknap Press, 2014.

Marc Solomon	*Winning Marriage: The Inside Story of How Same-Sex Couples Took on the Politicians and Pundits—and Won.* Lebanon, NH: ForeEdge, 2014.
Bret Stephens	*America in Retreat: The New Isolationism and the Coming Global Disorder.* New York: Sentinel, 2014.
Cass R. Sunstein	*Why Nudge?: The Politics of Libertarian Paternalism.* New Haven, CT: Yale University Press, 2014.
William Voegeli	*The Pity Party: A Mean-Spirited Diatribe Against Liberal Compassion.* New York: Broadside Books, 2014.
Thomas E. Woods Jr.	*Real Dissent: A Libertarian Sets Fire to the Index Card of Allowable Opinion.* Seattle, WA: CreateSpace, 2014.

Index

D

E

H

I

M

N

O

P

R

S

T

CPSIA information can be obtained
at www.ICGtesting.com
Printed in the USA
FFOW05n1146120116

9 780737 775358